THE FACE WITHIN

HOW TO CHANGE YOUR UNCONSCIOUS BLUEPRINT

Sue Lester

Copyright © 2013 by Susan Meree Lester

All rights reserved. No part of this book may be reproduced by any mechanical, photographic, or electronic process, or in the form of a phonographic recording; nor may it be stored in a retrieval system, transmitted, or otherwise be copied for public or private use – other than for "fair use" as brief quotations embodied in articles and reviews – without prior written permission from the author.

Disclaimer: The author of this book does not dispense medical advice or prescribe the use of any technique as a form of treatment for physical, emotional or medical problems without the advice of a physician, either directly or indirectly. The intent of the author is only to offer information of a general nature to help you in your quest for emotional and spiritual well-being. In the event you use any of the information in this book for yourself, which is your constitutional right, the author and publisher assume no responsibility for your actions. Although the examples and stories are based on actual case studies, for privacy reasons names, events and identifying elements have been changed, and for clarity and brevity, some are a combination of case studies. It is acknowledged that by changing one person's story it may inadvertently become similar to another's. This is unintentional and simply confirmation of the commonality in peoples' lives. Any suggestion of self-healing is not intended to replace the advice of your medical practitioner. Stories from the author's personal life are obviously interpreted from within her own reality and therefore naturally will differ from another participant's reality and memories. That does not make either party wrong.

This edition published May 2013 by:
Growing Content Pty Ltd
Telephone: 61 7 3103 2679
Web: www.growingcontent.com.au
Email: info@growingcontent.com.au

Editor: Alli Grant and Phyl Grant (www.alliandgenine.com)
Layout and design: Johanna Jensen (gojodesign@hotmail.com)
Book cover design: Ryan McDonald-Smith (www.Youniquecreation.com)
Illustrations: Liane Barker (www.InspiredBusinessDesign.com.au)
Cover photography: Peter Nink

ISBN paperback: 978-0-9875014-0-0
ISBN online: 978-0-9875014-1-7

Dedication

For my parents, Ken and Meree Lester, who have always loved and encouraged me to live my own life.

And a special heartfelt thank you to Peter Nink, for believing in me even before I did.

* * * * *

"The only difference between stumbling blocks and stepping stones is the way in which you use them."

Unknown

CONTENTS

A NOTE FROM THE AUTHOR	1
INTRODUCTION	5
ESSENTIAL PRE-READING EXERCISE	7
ONE THE INSPIRATION – THE FACE WITHIN REVEALED	13
TWO STORIES OF CHANGING FACES	19
THREE INTRODUCING YOUR CAPTAIN AND CREW	33
FOUR WHOSE WORLD IS IT? MAPPING YOUR REALITY	37
FIVE RECLAIMING YOUR PERSONAL POWER INCLUDING FINANCIAL FREEDOM	57
SIX POWER VALUES: YOUR TRUE DRIVERS	77
SEVEN PUTTING THE 'I' BACK INTO YOUR LIFE	95
EIGHT DE-STRESS FOR SUCCESS	107
NINE PAIN AND DIS-EASE	133
TEN WEIGHING HEAVILY IN YOUR MIND	153
ELEVEN ARE YOU UNCONSCIOUSLY BLOCKING CONCEPTION?	167
TWELVE RELATIONSHIPS REFRESHED	179
THIRTEEN NEXT STEPS: HOW TO LET GO AND GROW	195
KEY POINT SUMMARY	203
REFERENCES & RECOMMENDATIONS	211
TESTIMONIALS	215
ABOUT THE AUTHOR	221
NEXT RELEASES	227

"*The power of intuitive understanding
will protect you from harm
until the end of your days.*"

Lao Tzu

A NOTE FROM THE AUTHOR

What makes your heart sing? I'm excited about people, like you and me, living rich and fulfilling lives. What does 'rich and fulfilling' mean for you? I absolutely love adventurous travel, especially in culturally different or naturally beautiful areas. My experiences walking across the Simpson Desert with 16 camels, being charged by a silverback gorilla in the Republic of Congo, dodging hippos while canoeing the Zambezi River, navigating over a high altitude landslide in Nepal, and swimming with sea lions in Galapagos Islands, are all part of my story, the song of my heart. When I'm not allowing it, I feel out of sorts, unfulfilled, small and resentful.

As far back as I remember, I had planned to explore the world, to teach, and have a family. Although I did teach and travel, along the way I allowed myself to be ambushed by unrequited love, which resulted in low self-esteem, flowing on to a series of poorly paid, high stress jobs, no children and eight years in an abusive relationship. I also punished myself with rheumatoid arthritis and vomiting tension headaches. I became very good at saying "Yes" and "No" in all the wrong places: all fantastic research which helps me connect with and better serve now, but seriously, you really don't need to go there yourself! And if you've been there, or far worse as many have, know you can leave it behind, just as I did.

Most importantly, I've learnt how best to adapt to change, to learn and move on, and the value of self-value. We humans are the most amazing creatures, almost unlimited in our ability to adapt, change, grow and evolve. I named my business Growing Content because that's what I wanted for myself as well as for you. I realised my purpose is to be a catalyst of change, and allowing that makes my heart sing too.

When I resigned from paid employment to launch my own business, one month after signing up for my first mortgage, I had little more than an unwavering belief in the amazing results the techniques I'd learnt could achieve. I was just so excited about helping women struggling with unexplained infertility to release the unconscious fears blocking conception. That was my initial focus, which widened as people came to me asking for the same release from emotional pain and self-sabotage – provided I didn't make them pregnant! Resigning was a lot like jumping off a cliff hoping I could fly. Fortunately, I found my wings before I hit the bottom. It wasn't a logical, sensible, grown-up decision by any account, but boy did it feel so right!

I am extremely and humbly grateful for five people in particular whose belief in me made it easier to find and use my wings. Peter Nink, my new-ish boyfriend back then, life partner now, encouraged me 100 per cent and was willing to catch me if needed. Mary Melling and Peter Delaney believed in my passion, potential and professionalism enough to allow me to join their clinic practitioner team. Leah Barton, my coach at the time, sharpened my focus. Benjamin J. Harvey, my coach and mentor since, refined and strengthened my flight technique.

It has been such a pleasure and privilege over the years to be allowed into my clients' most private selves to help them let go and grow. I've learnt so much about myself, and life in general, from each, which in turn has helped so many more. We're all growing and evolving together. (I've lost count how many times I've been working with a client, then had the thought, "Hmm, make note to self"!)

The day my senses were opened to the existence of our individual unconscious blueprints was a blessing, one I could have easily missed if I hadn't been comfortable enough in my own professional skin to go left-field. Actually, ego aside, perhaps I had missed it many times before, simply unaware! Well, now I am aware, and I use that awareness with every client. The purpose of writing this book is to share it with you too, because I know I can't work individually with everyone on this planet of ours in one lifetime.

A NOTE FROM THE AUTHOR

The difference it has made, and continues to make, in people's lives is more than heart-warming. It's my legacy. I know for each person I help there is a positive ripple-on effect out to all in their lives; family, friends, colleagues, strangers in chance meetings, and also generationally, from their children to their children and beyond. Frankly, I need my butt kicked for not finishing this book sooner!

Know you are worthy. You are enough. You are loved. Everything you need is inside. You just need to learn how to ask, listen and act. If you wish, I can help you with this part of your journey, to clear your head trash and smooth your path into growing content.

"Don't go through life, grow through life."

Eric Butterworth

INTRODUCTION

I remember how I felt that moment. I think I was around 28 years old. I had the thunderbolt realisation that, although I was officially an adult, I actually didn't know everything, and sometimes didn't know what action to take. Like many children, I was conditioned by comments such as, "When you're grown up then you can do that. You can have it your way when you're the adult. Don't question me – I'm the adult and you're just a child". I came to believe that once I became an adult I would automatically know what to do in every situation, and I would have total control over my life.

Ironically, prior to the thunderbolt realisation, I had actually been living my life to those assumptions, making choices that felt right to me, even when 'sensible' people gasped and shook their heads. By the age of 25 I had studied at two universities, lived in four cities, married, divorced, created and healed rheumatoid arthritis in my body, turned down a career promotion rarely offered to women, and headed off alone to Egypt for what turned out to be three years of travelling Europe, the USA and Africa.

After the thunderbolt I lost my self-belief somehow, and doubts and fears moved in, staying for well over a decade. They led into an abusive relationship and poor career choices, until I re-learnt that yes, I could have control over my life, if I chose.

In the modern world of so many choices, it is easy to be overwhelmed to the point of believing you have limited or even no choice about how you live your life: the job you have, your partner, where you live, your weight, or how you spend your time and money. You answer "No" to yourself on behalf of others, before even asking your question. Truly understanding that you do have a choice, that you can step into your personal power, can be both intensely liberating and terrifying.

Have you seen the picture of a little ginger kitten looking into a mirror and seeing a lion reflected back? The caption says, "It's how you see yourself that counts". Importantly, that little kitten can grow into an adult version of the lion. He's not trying to be an eagle.

This book takes that concept from the external to the internal. It's how you see yourself inside, your internal unconscious blueprint™, that really counts. Your unconscious blueprint™ determines how you interact with yourself, in relationships at home and at work, and with the outside world as a whole.

If you wish to gain maximum mileage out of your time investment in reading this book, complete the Essential Pre-Reading Tasks that follow.

✏️ ESSENTIAL PRE-READING EXERCISE

Are you a gobbler or a savourer of books? If you are a savourer, you already know this, so please bear with me for a few lines while I make a firm and essential request of my fellow gobblers. Gobblers; perhaps like me you've been blessed with the ability to speed read. Maybe you're just eager to cram as much into life as quickly as possible, but just this once, please do this exercise below right now, before continuing on.

No, of course you won't be struck by the wrath of God or get 1,000 years bad luck if you don't. You will, however, miss out on some magic later on. And yes, you are kidding yourself if you pretend you'll come back and do the exercises later when you re-read the book slowly – you know a new title from that pile waiting on your bedside table or in your e-reader will seduce you instead.

So, savourers and gobblers both, please read the next couple of lines then close your eyes and don't think of a green dog. Open your eyes and write down the breed of dog here ('mongrel' or 'bitsa' are acceptable answers too):

_____

Write the shade of green here (for example, light / puke / grassy / dark):

_____

[Stop reading and do the exercise now.]

Okay, that was a little test to prove to yourself that you can see, or imagine you can see, images, and in colour too. Yes, it's perfectly okay if your image wasn't sharply focussed – mine rarely are. If you saw in black and white or sepia, imagine what green your dog could be. If you didn't actually see an image, if you had, what sort of green dog would you have seen? It was also a test for gobblers to prove they can stop and fully participate, if they wish.

Now, this is the first essential exercise. Once again, read the next few lines then close your eyes and bring up a picture of yourself. Have a look at it, notice if more than one image flashes up. Open your eyes then write down how old you are in that image here:

_____

_____

If you saw more than one image of yourself, write down the other age / ages here in the order you noticed them:

_____

_____

Here is the second essential exercise. If you had just been handed that picture you saw of yourself, how would you describe the person in it, for example his / her mood, character, appearance etc?:

_____

_____

[Stop reading and do the exercise now.]

The third essential part is here, identifying your personal Time Stream. Read the next few lines then close your eyes (don't worry, this is the last of the eye closing for quite a while) and think of where you'd point to, if you needed to point to your past. Allow yourself to point to your past. Write down the direction you pointed (for example, in front, to the left, two o'clock, or wherever it is for you):

_____

_____

[Stop reading and do the exercise now.]

ESSENTIAL PRE-READING EXERCISE

This time when you close your eyes, please imagine where you'd point if you needed to point to your future. Write down the direction you pointed here:

_____

_____

Close your eyes and just be aware that your past and future are connected in some way, and notice if that connection goes through you, around you, in front of you, above you or somewhere else, and write it down here:

_____

_____

Write down what your connection looks like in both form and colour, for example, a thin, black line or purple-orange smoke. If you feel you can't see it clearly, no matter, just imagine you can. What is the look of your unique Time Stream, colour and shape? Write it down here, knowing there is no wrong answer:

_____

_____

[Stop reading and do these now, if you haven't already. If you have, well done you! You're set to gain an enormous amount from this book.]

I'll be explaining how you'll be using this information to create change in yourself later in the book. For the moment, just trust you've done exactly what you need to do right now to start your cogs of change turning at the deepest unconscious level, where all lasting change occurs.

BONUS 1: *Email me at info@growingcontent.com.au with 'The Face Within Tasks' in the subject line, your name, current age, plus the information you wrote above, and I'll send you a Personal Power Boost webinar recording, and put you into the monthly draw for a free 30-minute telephone Unconscious Blueprint Revision session.*

BONUS 2: *Go to www.growingcontent.com.au and sign up to my monthly newsletter to get your free copy of my e-book, Win-Win Loving: Your Guide To Even More Loving Relationships and Harmonious Homes.*

ESSENTIAL PRE-READING EXERCISE

"You can't start the next chapter of your life if you keep re-reading the last one."

Unknown

ONE.

THE INSPIRATION – THE FACE WITHIN REVEALED

He sat before me, casually yet smartly dressed, hands trembling as he described the stab of fear he felt each time his telephone rang. With every ring he was more certain something dreadful had happened to one of his children. His unfounded but gut-wrenching reaction was intensifying day by day. It was affecting his ability to function in his busy daily life, creating stress in his relationship with his second wife and with his children. The more he tried to help and look out for them, the more his children resisted, aggravating his anguish to the point where it was consuming his life.

As I watched Robert share his story, I had a flash of inspiration, the kind that sounds illogical, even ridiculous, but is so insistent it simply has to be acted on.

"Robert, this might sound strange, but would you mind closing your eyes for a moment?

"Thank you.

"Now, in your mind, bring up a picture of your eldest child. Can you see her?

"Good. What age is she in that picture?"

Robert's answer was that his daughter was six years old. We repeated the exercise for each child, and they were all between six and 10 years old. I knew Robert was in his early 70's, so how old was his eldest daughter really?

She was 46 years old!

This explained everything. Of course you worry about a six-year-old going to live in the concrete jungle alone. Of course you don't send a 10-year-old to work on a mine site without a concern. Absolutely you help your eight-year-old with project research and offer advice on every aspect of his life. And as an adult, you want your parents to treat you as such, to have faith and pride in your ability to run your own life successfully. Understandably there was tension with his adult children. Robert's second wife had only ever known his children as adults, so that's how she treated them. She was nonplussed and frustrated by Robert's unnecessary over-protectiveness.

The following session, we updated his internal images of his children, and he also updated the photos of them in his wallet and in his home. (By "we" I mean my client and I, as I use "do with" rather than "do to" processes.) I was curious about why his internal images were so out-of-date, particularly since he did see them in person at least every month or so. Robert confessed that he felt he'd been a dreadful father, and husband for that matter. During their younger years, he was frequently partying, indulging in long, boozy business lunches, and was rarely home sober for them. By the time their daughter was 10, his wife had had enough and divorced him, taking full custody of the children. Robert's most emotionally-charged memories of his children were from that time, saturated in guilt and remorse.

Interestingly, Robert's own internal image of himself was in his 40's, from the period when he finally fully appreciated what he had lost and how he had neglected his children. That was the time he put a concerted effort into reconnecting with and getting to know his children. We updated his internal image to his early 60's, to a time he felt wiser, happier, but still fit, strong and active. It's not necessary for your internal image (your unconscious blueprint™) to match your chronological age. In fact, in my experience, a younger image, as long as it is positive and within 10 or so years, manifests in more energy and activity. We also adjusted Robert's personal time stream so he could more easily leave his past where it belonged and focus on living in the present.

The following session he reported nothing to report. All was fine. Nothing unusual had happened – just his usual, busy life. So I inquired whether his telephone had rung at all during the week. He looked bemused and confused. Well, of course it had. And yes, he'd spoken with his eldest son and had a good, long talk about things in general. Then the light literally went on in his face. He suddenly realised he hadn't stressed about the phone ringing even once, and that his son had responded warmly to the relaxed man-to-man attitude from his father.

In subsequent sessions we used a variety of NLP (Neuro Linguistic Programming) processes to clear the excess of negative emotions such as anger, fear and guilt out of his system, so Robert could increase his personal power by easily managing his emotional state. For example, instead of frequently erupting in anger or frustration, he was able to choose to be assertive instead. His business and personal relationships improved significantly.

When his youngest son asked, yet again, for money, instead of instantly feeling the surge of guilt and reaching for his wallet, Robert was able to think clearly about whether he really was helping his son out, or simply enabling financial irresponsibility. Sometimes the very best way to help someone is to say "No" to them. It creates a necessity, and perhaps urgency, for them to start taking responsibility for their own lives: to step up, out of the pity pit or puddle of poo, and stretch and grow. Yes, it can be uncomfortable for everyone concerned, but think of it as growing pains. Ultimately, your wisdom will be seen as tough love and appreciated. Once Robert's son eventually stopped getting angry about the money-flow drying up, he started treating his father with more respect, and settled into more steady employment.

Robert's wife sent me a note thanking me for saving their marriage. From her perspective, her husband was finally acting rationally, and was much more relaxed, loving and present for her. This last point was significant – remember Robert's internal images were all from a time pre-second wife, and his time stream past was in front of him? So she was often literally invisible to him when he was consumed with worrying about his children, or wallowing in his guilt.

In the years since my inspiration with Robert, I've made investigating clients' internal images of themselves and others, and the location of their time stream, essential exploratory elements for both clinic and coaching clients. The variety is endlessly fascinating, and the life-changing results from making adjustments both highly-gratifying and humbling.

In the following pages I'll be sharing some of these illuminating stories. I'll also explain how you can increase your effectiveness in your life, improve your relationships and business success, and most importantly, feel great about being you. High self-esteem really is the key to a successful life, whatever 'successful' means to you. No matter what you change externally, your weight, your partner, your hair, your job or your address, it is your internal self-worth and your unconscious blueprint™ which dictate your level of satisfaction and joy. Your 'face within' matters.

So let's move on to the next chapter and some examples of how others have discovered the significant difference that changing their unconscious blueprint™ can make to their lives.

KEY POINTS

» **You have an unconscious blueprint™ which can be affecting your life negatively.**

» **Changing your unconscious blueprint™ changes your self-esteem and confidence.**

» **Your unconscious blueprint™ of others dictates your relationship with them.**

» **Guilt chains you to your past.**

THE INSPIRATION: THE FACE WITHIN REVEALED

"Everybody is a genius. But if you judge a fish by its ability to climb a tree, it will live its whole life believing it is stupid."

Albert Einstein

TWO.
STORIES OF CHANGING FACES

Disclaimer: Although the following stories are based on actual case studies, for privacy reasons names, events and identifying elements have been changed, and for clarity and brevity, some are a combination of case studies. It is acknowledged that by changing one person's story it may inadvertently become similar to another's. This is unintentional and simply confirmation of the commonality in people's lives.

* * * * *

EMMA

I gazed across the table in admiration at the sleek-haired, smartly-dressed, slim, young woman. Emma spoke confidently, projecting her voice through the coffee lounge babble, and her dark eyes sparkled as she smiled and shared her latest news. When Emma first came to see me, at the behest of a concerned relative, she sidled into the room in a tired, baggy t-shirt, crumpled shorts and cheap rubber thongs. Her hair looked as if she'd just tumbled out of bed, which she had at 11:00am. She mumbled about how her days were often spent eating and crying on the sofa, her nights being taunted and roughly handled by her boyfriend.

Emma's childhood read like the definitive collection of child abuse stories from a child psychology textbook. It seemed like everything that could happen did, except that she managed to live despite the suicide attempts, with mind and body relatively intact. Interestingly, Emma had a very strong moral code, but because no one in her life matched her values and her sense of right and wrong, she thought she was the mad misfit. She was an outcast in her own social circle because she was honest. She didn't do one night stands, drugs or steal. Despite feeling wretched in her relationship and gaining new bruises every day, she didn't label her boyfriend as "abusive" or her situation as "domestic violence". Compared with what she had grown up with, this was much better so must be "normal".

Emma's internal image was of a four-year-old, and she was 24 years old at the time we worked together. She said the age of four was the last time she felt safe. Unfortunately, it meant she often responded to the world emotionally as a four-year-old, sulking and feeling very insecure, clinging to her boyfriend despite his behaviour. After this was revealed, Emma confessed a few years earlier that a psychologist had told her she had the emotional age of a five-year-old, so it made sense to her. Her time stream was knotted up inside her, and that made sense too, daily reliving her past and having very little sense of a future beyond a few days. Emma saw the sense of having her past behind her and was keen to create a future worth looking forward to, so she willingly followed my guidance and adjusted her time stream into the optimum position, finding it easy to lock into place.

She was my first case where the internal image didn't update immediately to the desired age, in this case her chronological age. Emma said she didn't want to let go of that sense of safety and couldn't relate it to her current situation. The compromise was 16 years old, which was the most recent time she felt above the misery and able to say "No" to abuse. Since then I have found it not uncommon for someone with an internal image of under 10 to need to change in increments, almost as if they need to spend some time as a teenager before becoming an adult.

After a series of sessions, Emma suddenly made significant changes sooner than I had expected. She announced she had left her boyfriend, was moving out of town, and had started applying for career-orientated jobs, such as the armed forces. At that point I re-checked her internal image and it was up to her chronological age of its own accord. The work we'd done together redefining her identity, self-worth and confidence, plus teaching boundary setting and building self-trust had paid off significantly.

She is now on a retail career fast-track, after initially starting at entry level and being promoted through the ranks to trainee manager within seven months.

ROSEMARY

Did you ever experience bullying at high school? Perhaps you were able to shrug it off fight back? Perhaps you found it all too much to resist? Rosemary was quiet, plump, spoke with an accent, and found it very difficult to cope with her high school bullies. Now, as an adult in her 40's, she was being bullied, or on good days ignored, by her teenage children. She was bored, very overweight, lonely and felt disconnected from everyone, including her husband. Despite the potential for a great deal of change in her life, Rosemary came to me only because she needed the confidence to get a job (her first ever!) so she could have her own money to spend as she pleased.

Rosemary's internal image was that of a 14-year-old. She was eager to update it to a healthy and confident 40-year-old. We repositioned her past where it belonged, and ensured her future was stretching out into the distance in front of her. I taught her about personal power, how to tell the difference between intuition and self-doubt, boundary setting and maintenance, and helped her change her beliefs in her intelligence and her potential.

She had regularly met with a group of neighbours for years, but confessed she had never felt comfortable, just obligated to go and too shy to refuse. Shaking her head in amazement, she said that day she had looked around the room and for the first time noticed they were all women in their 40's, just like her. Rosemary said she had suddenly felt like she belonged. Half an hour after that, one neighbour was talking about a job vacancy and Rosemary found the confidence to speak up and ask how she could apply. She was amazed and delighted when the woman commented that Rosemary would be perfect for the role.

Within a fortnight, Rosemary had her dream job working as a disability carer; admittedly not everyone's dream job, but Rosemary loved the connection with staff and clients, the sense of purpose, and of course, the money ... her money. However, she said, "I can't believe they're paying me to do this job – I love it so much, I'd do it for free". So in the end, having her own money wasn't the answer. In fact, it rarely is. What we really want are the feelings associated with money and what it can be exchanged for: security, safety and feeling special or unique. We really want peace of mind, knowing that we are okay and so are our loved ones.

On the home front, Rosemary was speaking up and laying down boundaries for her teenagers, and although it looked like very slow progress, she was pleased with herself. The only problem was that she still felt disconnected from her husband, irritated by him. Checking her internal image of her husband we found the reason – she saw him as one of those annoying teenage boys – loud, showing off and totally incomprehensible, just like one of her son's friends. Once we updated that, she was able to see him on all levels as the loving, intelligent, adult man he is: someone a grown-up woman like herself would like to be romantic with. He was delighted!

HEIDI

Not everyone is as eager to change, as you might expect. Making change naturally involves letting go of the familiar for the unknown. Some people can feel very secure in their uncomfortable rut. You probably know someone who complains bitterly about something or someone but doesn't take that one action that would resolve the problem. They say things like, "Ah well, better the devil you know ...", or, "I couldn't possibly. What if ...?", or "It's okay for you, but I ...". They successfully argue for their limitations.

Heidi was suffering from intense anxiety, particularly around two issues. One was her dogs, to the point she fretted about leaving them to go to work each day. They naturally picked up her anxiety and became stressed and fretful themselves, to the tune of hundreds of dollars in vet bills. Anxiety can affect dogs in particular because they are pack animals, and (ideally, though unfortunately not always) the human owner is the pack leader. If the pack leader senses danger and responds in fear, there must be serious danger around, even if the rest of the pack can't see, hear or smell it themselves, in the same way children pick up on their parents' anxieties and tension. Cats, of course, would simply leave home until their anxious owner calmed down, or would permanently shift residence if necessary. Very pragmatic animals, cats.

Her second issue was the reason for her visit. She said she desperately wanted to have a child, could see their happy family behind their white picket fence, but was simply terrified of getting pregnant, and even more so of giving birth. She had recently miscarried and was torn between blissful relief and stabbing guilt at feeling relief. Her husband controlled their finances, and although he would pay the dogs' hefty vet bills, he would not pay for his wife to seek help for something "just in her mind". They hadn't made the connection between her anxiety and the dogs' stress.

Pre-pubescent girls often have the happy family images and love playing with babies. They are rarely aware of the physiological details and psychological impact of pregnancy and birth. Many would never have seen a birth, let alone a positive one, apart from scenes of some poor woman screaming and swearing in a TV hospital sitcom. The majority of clients I've worked with on unexplained infertility issues have had pre-pubescent internal images and have updated them in stages during our work together.

Heidi's internal image was 10 years old, which explained the conflict between happy families and her perceived reality of pregnancy and birth. It also explained why she was comfortable with the degree of control her husband had assumed in managing most aspects of their life together. Heidi asked if she could make her change the next session when she wasn't feeling so tired, but sadly, though not surprisingly, she chose not to return.

JAMES

At the start of our coaching program, James had initially rated his relationship as zero out of 10 (which he agreed to modify to half as he was actually in a relationship), his small business as three out of 10, and his self-esteem and mental health as two out of 10. At the end of our 12-month coaching agreement, we remeasured James's self-evaluation and he rated his relationship as eight out of 10, and said that for the first time in at least 25 years he had felt sad rather than relieved seeing his long suffering partner, Bill, off at the airport to return to his job at the mines. He rated his business as seven out of 10 and growing, and his mental health as eight out of 10 and improving.

James had grown up in England as the only child of older parents. He was over-indulged, but in return he was expected to achieve highly in everything he did. Consequently, nothing he did was ever good enough in his own eyes, and often in the eyes of his parents as well, especially his mother. He was bitterly disappointed in himself. That played out in how he treated his partner, Bill, and also his staff, whom he called his "little girls" and struggled to trust. James's internal image was 13 years old and his time stream past was directly in front of him where he could easily wallow in his regrets and old hurts. For James, moving past the time he first acknowledged he was homosexual was significant, and learning to love himself paramount to rebuilding his self-esteem and relationship with Bill.

Although James's business started to improve in line with his self-esteem, progress seemed slower than expected. The main issue identified was high staff turnover, due in part to James sacking staff for laziness and dishonesty, and because staff worth retaining due to boredom and resentment. It is probable that James had started calling his staff his "little girls" when he was feeling insecure in his 13-year-old internal image. He now had to update those images too and see his staff for the young, and not-so-young, capable women they were.

They became his "team members" and were invited to contribute at the new weekly team meetings, and to the development of the new staff training system. James now felt more comfortable delegating to more experienced team members. This reduced his stress levels and freed up time and head space for regular business development planning. His staff felt more appreciated and were able to develop their skills and engage in more stimulating work. Those who didn't like the new accountability and key performance indicators soon left, which created a further positive shift in the workplace culture.

ANDREW

"I feel like I'm constantly battling with myself. I'm not even sure who I am anymore. I used to be so motivated, on top of the world, and now I'm just lost and every day is getting harder. I love my wife and kids, but some days I think I should have stayed single."

Andrew had made a mid-life career change from a highly mentally and physically challenging but exciting position in a national organisation, which involved long periods of travel, to running his own franchised business. The reason for his career change was to be home to see his young children grow up and keep his marriage intact. Now his wife was complaining he was there physically but not emotionally for her and their children. Andrew was also experiencing conflict with the promising young man he had hired with a view to training as a manager for his next branch.

His internal image initially seemed very positive. As a 40-year-old his internal image was of himself in his 20's, at a time of his peak physical and mental fitness when he felt he could conquer the world, and was doing so in his choice of career. Further exploration revealed that at that time he was also extremely egotistical, arrogant, sexist and generally emotionally cold. These were quite different values (and attitude) to the present Andrew who is a compassionate, empathetic family man who provides wonderful customer service by really listening to his clients and going the extra mile.

In this case, we constructed a new internal image combining his focussed energy, enthusiasm and confidence of the past with his gained maturity, experience, tolerance and wisdom. To achieve the balance Andrew and his family wanted, we developed a structure for that focussed energy to be most effective. His weekly schedule included time for himself, his marriage, his children, his health, his business planning, and day-to-day business activities. The results quickly materialised with his business becoming number one in the state, even though he had stopped taking work home and was spending those hours playing with his kids, romancing his wife, and working out at the gym instead.

The next issue was the conflict with his "young muck". Actually, he used a slightly different word, but "muck" will suffice in print. His internal image of this employee, Adam, was almost a caricature. Adam's neat, modern haircut became a coiffeur, his fashionable dress sense became "gay flamboyance", and the overall image was of a simpering fop.

In reality, Adam appeared to me as an intelligent, well-dressed, masculine man in his late 20's who was able to charm women when he chose. It was important for the sake of Andrew's business growth that we revise his internal image of Adam from "muck" to "buck". He was then able to train Adam effectively and feel comfortable delegating responsibility to him. Adam responded favourably to the new respectful and inclusive attitude of his boss, and they eventually started connecting on a friendship level.

JUDY, HARRY AND ROBYN

Sometimes, as in the cases of Judy, Harry and Robyn, where there wasn't an age discrepancy between chronological age and internal image, it was the image itself that reflected the problem.

Judy saw herself as her current age, which was 48, but also as fat, frumpy and unhappy. She therefore ate, dressed and acted like a fat and frumpy person. Judy made herself even more unhappy along the way with her negative self-talk. It could be argued that her internal image was a direct result of her dress sense and eating habits. However, she struggled to release her excess weight until we slimmed down her internal image, dressed it attractively and put a smile on its face. Of course, in Judy's case she needed other work with me to also improve her self-esteem and release the baggage of excess, negative emotions, such as anger and guilt, out of her system. She also needed to replace that venomous voice in her ear (her self-talk bitch) with one more encouraging and supportive.

Harry was unusual in that he saw himself as older, bent over and grey of face, in his 60's and unhealthy, rather than his true age of 54. He felt weighed down by the burdens of his life as he saw them, and it was only after we reframed and removed some of those burdens both in his mind and his reality that he willingly updated to a more energised and younger internal image. Prior to that, he indicated his preference to hurry to his grave to get this life over and done with, and had displayed suicidal tendencies. Harry is now actively turning his business around, rather than sitting wishing things were different and telling himself scary stories about Hopeless Harry.

Robyn saw herself as her current age of 42, but as weak, helpless, dependent and not terribly smart. This image matched beautifully to the role she had played throughout her years of marriage. However, it no longer served her now her husband had left for a prettier and much younger version. Her anger at her husband's behaviour ignited then fuelled her motivation to get serious about changing how she saw herself and lived the rest of her life.

She proved a delight to work with, being highly motivated. By the time we had gained enough leverage to be able to safely clear that excess anger, it really was like watching a butterfly emerge from a chrysalis. Robyn's renewed sense of self and self-worth opened her eyes to opportunities. Her new confidence and desire for revenge through success motivated her to grab those opportunities and build herself a new career. Although her original motivation was negatively powered, as she savoured her own successes she became motivated for her own sake because she loved her new role. Her ex-husband as an energy source was no longer needed, freeing her to attract more compatible men and connect on a more equal relationship footing.

Judith's summary of why she came to me was, "I want to figure out why, if I'm so smart, I am so poor?". Her life was that of a grasshopper, jumping from her original professional career to a series of ad-hoc businesses. She described herself as an entrepreneur, yet a series of less than successful businesses seemed more along the lines of get-rich-quickly schemes. They absolutely worked, but seemingly only for the entrepreneurs that created and crafted the schemes, not those like Judith who bought into them. Judith felt she was self-sabotaging due to her underlying poverty consciousness and wanted to rid herself of it before her next big project started.

At 64, Judith's unconscious blueprint™ was a ghostly image of an elderly woman in her 80's. This was hardly an empowering one for moving forward decisively into a new business venture. Judith said the image matched her feeling of being not quite here, of being disconnected and lost. She felt invisible at times, particularly in crowded places where people brushed past her in their hurry. Due to poor sleeping patterns, Judith had dark circles under her eyes and was carrying some extra weight which showed in her face, so she selected a photograph rather than the mirror to use for her unconscious blueprint™ update. The photo was a few years old but taken at a happier time, and was more in alignment with who, or rather how, she wanted to be.

Judith's personal time stream was wrapped around her, so that needed to be untangled and laid out in the optimum position, the past behind one shoulder, and the future stretching out in front. The next process in the change was to clean up her excess baggage, so we did an energetic cord cutting process which enabled her to identify the current negative connections with the past behaviours and self-identity, then cut and cleanse those connections. Interestingly, the negative connections were all with friends who had guided her investment in projects in the past three decades. Judith reported feeling "much lighter" after this process.

Between sessions, to increase her sense of being grounded and present, I gave her a task to commit to on a daily basis. That's the Senses Walk mentioned in Chapter 8, De-Stress for Success. This exercise is excellent for bringing yourself back to the present, which, of course, is the only moment that is real and the only moment we can act on that directly creates our future. For most of us 99.99 per cent of the time, in the present we are physically safe, so our adrenal system can slip back into idle, our heart rate can slow to a comfortable rhythm, our body's natural healing abilities can function more effectively, and much of the mental white noise stops. For Judith, it brought her back into her physical body and reconnected her with her physical sensory receptors so she felt "back". From that position she started doing her due diligence on opportunities rather than blindly accepting the fabulous vision presented as truth by her friends.

JACKIE

The labels we give ourselves reflect and reinforce our identity to ourselves and others. For example, if you label yourself as "just a mum", you not only immediately devalue your most important role as a mother, you've put yourself into a box separate from the working world. Jackie labelled herself as "just a disability carer". To me, caring for a disabled child, particularly your own as that is for life, is one of the most difficult jobs to do well, and I greatly admire the strength, resilience and spirit of those who do. So there was nothing "just" about Jackie, and part of her own unconscious needed to believe that, so changing her unconscious blueprint™ was quick and powerful. It freed her to finish her long-delayed studies and start a new career.

Jackie had also guiltily revealed how frustrated she was when her son with cerebral palsy cried and lashed out. His behaviour was becoming worse as he grew older, and her patience and energy was becoming more and more stretched. Interestingly, her unconscious blueprint™ of her son was of a three-month-old baby, yet he was now three years old. Once we updated that image and she started treating him like a three-year-old he blossomed. Not only did his frustrated behaviour stop, he started reaching milestones within his potential. At some level he had known he was a little boy, not a baby, even though his body was not letting him do what other little boys did. His playing up was his way of expressing that frustration.

In all of the cases above, the life changing shifts were from a combination of changing their unconscious blueprints™, clearing limiting self-beliefs, replacing disempowering habits, and increasing awareness of individual personal power and how we create our own reality. It isn't an event which shapes your life, it's your perception of that event, the meaning you give to it, and the consequent actions you take which have moulded the life you have now. In the following chapters we'll explore those concepts further, and will look at how you can apply that knowledge to your own life.

 TIME TO CHANGE EXERCISE: SELF-LABELLING

How are you labelling yourself? Are you "just a ..."? How are you labelling your spouse and your children? Labelling them as "just a ..." limits their potential, not only in your eyes, but also in theirs.

Write down your "just a ..." then at least 25 other things you are. You can include characteristics, skills, experience and qualifications.

Hint: If you are "just a ..." role, for example, "just a mum", then make sure you write the majority of other roles you play in your life and other people's lives. For example, home-manager, crowd controller, book-keeper, storeman, purchaser, fertility controller, wife, lover, friend, daughter, and so on.

If you are "just a ..." characteristic for example, "just a shy person", concentrate on all of your other characteristics. In other words, all that you are when you are forgetting to be shy. What are you like when your best friend calls? When your child breaks your favourite ornament? When you're in the mood for love?

Return the favour for anyone (or thing) you label "just a ..." , which will affect your emotional state and behaviour (note I refer to "things" as how you label and feel about your home, income, car, animal, plants etc). Notice how differently you feel about yourself, and them, afterwards. And yes, it is a serious exercise, but please have fun with it – let your imagination run wild! For example, if you empty the household bins, you can be a garbologist if you wish.

KEY POINTS

» Your unconscious blueprint™ can be delaying conception, stifling your business growth, sabotaging your relationships, and leaving you vulnerable to abuse.

» Your unconscious blueprint™ can easily be revised, with powerful flow-on effects.

» Labels are disempowering. No one or no-thing is "just a ...".

"It isn't an event which shapes your life, it's your perception of that event, the meaning you give to it, and the consequent actions you take which have moulded the life you have now."

Sue Lester

THREE.
INTRODUCING YOUR CAPTAIN AND CREW

To truly make lasting changes and take control back over your life, you need to work at both conscious and unconscious levels. In this chapter you'll discover more about how your conscious and unconscious minds work in together, and the reasons for your procrastination or self-sabotage.

So let's get into the explanation by introducing you to your captain and crew. Think of your body as your ship of life, with your captain on deck as your conscious mind, while below deck are your crew: that is, your unconscious (or subconscious) mind.

Now your captain can be on deck demanding, "Full steam ahead, and straight to Wealth Land!". (You can substitute the 'land' of your choice: baby, love, promotion, trim, taut and terrific etcetera.) However, what if below deck your crew (your unconscious mind) is saying, "Stuff that, we've tried it and it doesn't work!", or, "We're afraid, what if...?", or they are bickering about which is the best way to turn? Perhaps someone is in the corner with the rule book, saying, "Sorry, page 47 paragraph two says our family doesn't belong in Wealth Land". What do you think your ship will do? That's right – zigzag, stall or even turn around and go backwards!

It's essential to have alignment between your captain and crew, aka your conscious and unconscious minds, so your thoughts and actions match and you get the results you want. Remember, you always get results, just not necessarily the ones you wanted.

Alignment is essential, so when your captain sets up that savings account your crew doesn't get the urge to go shopping or to pay yourself last. Alignment so when your captain sets the alarm one hour earlier the night before so you can get up to exercise your crew doesn't hit the snooze button and start reminding you how cold and dark it is, and how tired you are. Alignment is essential so when that amazing opportunity appears you do your due diligence and take action quickly, rather than procrastinate until it's too late. Self-sabotage is turned into self-motivation.

Sometimes it can be more complicated than simply aligning your captain and crew. Just as in political parties, there can be different factions, or unconscious parts, with conflicting views on how best to proceed for the good of all. You'll recognise the existence of conflicting unconscious parts when you hear something like, "Hmm, I really don't know what to do. Part of me wants to, and part of me doesn't".

Those internal parts are formed over time through how we filter our experiences and the meaning we give to those events. More about filters soon, but for the moment consider that parts development as follows.

Imagine after your birth that your ship of life sets forth, navigating by the stars. It works well during the clear starry nights, but daytime and cloudy nights leave your ship unguided. Imagine the excitement when a crew member discovers the compass. At last a way to navigate, no matter what the weather! Still, in parts of the world the compass needle spins out of control, or is not quite so accurate, and care must be taken to store it correctly away from other magnetised objects. The majority are keen to adopt this new way, but part of the crew still believes in the stars as the best and only way to navigate. So your ship moves on, with some internal conflict on clear nights. Then someone discovers the GPS and there's wild excitement, though it has its drawbacks too and can end up simply an interesting paperweight if not calibrated and charged correctly. However wonderful the GPS seems, part of the crew still believes in the compass, and part still believes in navigating by the stars.

These parts of the crew disagree and fight amongst themselves, making decisions difficult, until a parts integration occurs. This is when all parts are guided to acknowledge they have the same highest positive intention for you, that is, arriving safely at your destination, and that by fighting they have actually been also stopping themselves from achieving their highest purpose. The crew are encouraged to acknowledge each other's strengths and find ways to work together as a harmonious whole. And the result is generally a feeling of calm wholeness, and the disappearance of much mental 'white noise'. Our beliefs and memories are generally stored as images, and often with associated emotions. Your internal image is the blueprint your crew or unconscious mind works from, and some people have two or even a series of internal images. Multiple images seem to occur when a person has more distinctive unconscious parts. You can see how a crew working from the blue print of a 14-year-old will respond differently to situations and make different decisions from a crew working from a blue print of a 40-year-old.

Over the remaining chapters we'll explore how these unconscious blueprints™ are formed, and then in Chapter 13 how they can be adjusted.

KEY POINTS

» **For smooth sailing through life, your captain (conscious mind) and crew (unconscious mind) must be in alignment.**

» **Memories, beliefs and your unconscious blueprint™ are stored as images in your unconscious mind and can be changed by adjusting the characteristics of those images.**

» **It is possible to have more than one unconscious blueprint™ of yourself.**

"'Worrying' is using your imagination to create something you don't want."

Abraham-Hicks

FOUR.
WHOSE WORLD IS IT? MAPPING YOUR REALITY

The first step in turning your self-sabotage into self-motivation is gaining the clarity as to who you are and why you respond to the world the way you do. It comes down to how your brain processes and filters the information coming in through all of your senses, as it is that filtering that determines what you focus on, and therefore what shows up in your life.

No one else has the same reality as you, because no one else has had exactly the same experiences from in the womb, and interpreted / filtered them in exactly the same way as you. What we filter for, what we focus on, is what we get and that determines our internal map of reality; how we see the world.

And everyone sees the world differently. This is a crucial point.

It's the reason why some people can rape, pillage, murder and throw bombs. They might be aware that officially their actions are wrong, but in their reality their behaviour has a justification. Once you truly understand this, it is actually quite liberating because you stop being hurt by other people's actions.

You may say things like, "How can he do that? I wouldn't. How can she say that? I wouldn't" and that's true. You wouldn't. But they're not you. So, once you stop expecting them to think and act and feel the way you do you can accept that that's who they are, this is who you are, and work around that. We only feel emotionally hurt when we are expecting people to act the way we would and when they don't it's painful. We take that to mean that they don't love us or they don't respect us, or whatever is applicable. That may be the case, but it also may not.

Remembering we have a choice about how we choose to interpret and give meaning to information is crucial at this point. Often checking in with the person to ascertain if your interpretation matches theirs is the quickest way to clarify and resolve issues. Unfortunately for many people, agonising over a range of potential meanings for days, weeks, years, is preferable to being courageously vulnerable and actually asking for clarity. Uncertainty can entertain hope and wishful thinking.

Clarity shines the bright light of reality and makes the way forward clear, even when it is not what one might wish to see. The assumption is, of course, that the recipient of your questioning was brave enough to tell the truth, rather than hide behind polite, superficial reassurances.

For some narrow thinkers, theirs is the only right interpretation, and going over and over the perceived injustice shores up their underlying low self-esteem with feelings of moral superiority. You may have experienced this: he picks at a scab over and over until it becomes infected, the pus builds up until the pain and pressure gets too much and he explodes, spraying those concerned with his pus. Totally gross ... and totally unnecessary.

INTERPRETING INFORMATION

The following diagram illustrates how our brain processes the information coming in through all of our senses, day and night, because, of course, our senses don't sleep when we do. It shows how the filtering affects our focus and reality, and therefore how we feel emotionally and physically, how we behave and the reason we get the results we do.

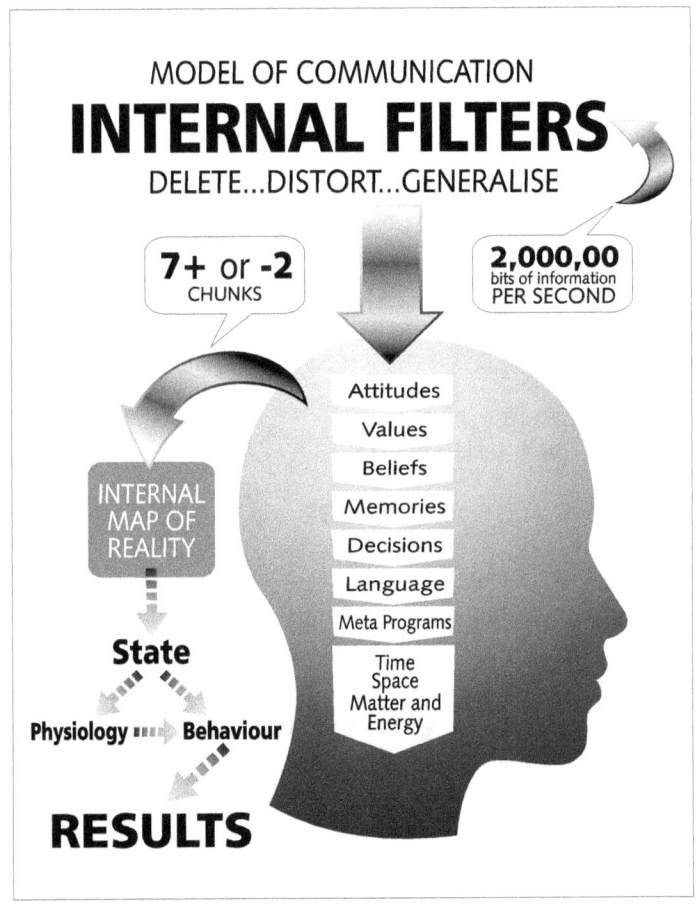

There is so much information flooding into our six senses, particularly in technologically-immersed cities, that our conscious mind would go into total overload trying to process it all. Our brain has evolved the Reticular Activating System (R.A.S.). One of its functions is to filter, then decide what remains conscious and what gets stored in the unconscious. Our internal filters which are deleting, distorting and generalising the approximately 2,000,000 bits of information per second in allow approximately seven chunks, or 126 bits, of information through (*Flow:*

The Psychology of Optimal Experience by Mihaly Csikszentmihalyi). How we filter shapes our reality, and therefore how we communicate and relate, barely survive or thrive.

In earlier tribal hunter-gatherer days, the man's focus was primarily on hunting, particularly once he had a mate, so his sharp focus was on signs to indicate where the prey was. Meanwhile, the woman was focussing on signs of a different form, that is, where the best fruit, roots, seeds, eggs etcetera were found, where her children were. She also was tuned to signs of danger, whether from predators or from her mate's withdrawal of protection. That's where the female talent for multitasking, imagining multiple scenarios and second-guessing male intentions, formed – perhaps!

Let's explore the filtering further.

DELETE

Deleting is not seeing or hearing something that either you are not expecting or not focussing on. For example, walking into a cafe, a single woman will notice all the attractive men in the room, while her happily married friend is focussed on finding a vacant table and perusing the menu. As another example, you might not notice a friend has changed her hair colour or is not wearing glasses.

DISTORT

An example of distortion is Denise being in a relationship that everyone else sees as toxic, and she is distorting the meaning of Henry's words and behaviours to match what she wants to believe. She distorts his behaviour to match her definition of love. Likewise, we grow up and leave home, and on our return our parents treat us like the 15-year-olds we used to be. They distort the woman back into the more familiar teenager. When we allow ourselves to be slotted back into childhood identity boxes, our resentment builds and tempers flare. We also are not allowing our family to get to know us as we truly are now. Likewise, you may not be recognising the changes they have made either.

GENERALISE

The third function of the filters is to generalise, so we don't have to keep learning individual items. This is extremely useful as once we learn what a chair is, for example, anywhere we go in the world we can sit down. We also generalise about places, their desirability or otherwise: "Sydney is such a hole!", and often this is based on our own filtered experiences or those of others, rather than the current state of that place. It may be true for a small part, but not the whole. We generalise about people, lumping them into groups according to race, religion, gender, age and occupation. The consequence is that we then treat one person as part of that generalised group, rather than as the individual she is. Unnecessarily excluding or inappropriately including, for example automatically trusting a pale-skinned man more than a dark skinned man or vice versa, can occur.

Most importantly, we generalise about ourselves, our abilities and behaviour, and in doing so are programming ourselves for success or failure. Have you noticed how we all love to be right? If you tell yourself, over and over, that you could never public speak well because you always forget your words and turn red, what will happen as you stand up to deliver your message? Exactly! You forget your words and turn red, as self-programmed, and then you can rightfully say, "See, I told you so. I knew that would happen. It always does!".

"Never" and "always" are clear signs of generalisations which aren't true 100 per cent of the time. If you want to ramp up the intensity of a disagreement, tell the other side they "always" or "never" do something. The obvious unfairness and incorrectness of your statement will push their fire-up button immediately.

Parents and teachers need to be very careful about what generalisations and labels they apply to children in their care as they can become self-fulfilling prophecies. I noticed this in every school I taught at. For example, "Pippa *always* struggles in maths ... Adam *never* sits still ... Jason *always* fights with his brother ... Gina *never* eats vegetables ... Harry is *always* late ... You *always* need to keep an eye on Tom ... Jill *is* the bright one" (implying her other siblings are dull). Particularly in the Imprint Period, in uteroto until seven years old, children are forming their self-identity and values based on what the most powerful people in their lives, parents and adults, tell and show them. Remember your tone, physiology and actions convey your true message.

So, to recap, we have information coming in through all our senses being deleted, distorted and generalised through our unique set of filters, determining how we experience and interpret our environment. How we interpret the world creates our personal reality and determines our emotional state which affects our physiology. This determines our behaviour, and therefore our results.

When Gillian misinterpreted a comment from her employee, Jack, she made a decision he was disrespectful and untrustworthy. This was based on her previous experience of similar verbal interactions and her current level of self-esteem. From that point, Jack's actions, words, facial expressions and body language were interpreted as further signs of disrespect and untrustworthiness. Jack struggled to be seen and treated differently, but in the end it was easier to slip into that role than continue to struggle or leave. What Gillian focussed on became her reality.

Similarly, in our education system students get labelled in the staffroom, and they are met each fresh year with their new teacher's pre-conceived expectations of their behaviour, intelligence levels and character. A new environment becomes the only chance of a fresh start. There's a reason office politics can have an uncanny resemblance to schoolyard politics.

Throughout this period, Gillian's stress and protective anger levels rose even more, as did Jack's frustration and hurt, rippling out across the workplace and into their private lives. Fifty-two-year-old Gillian's internal image of herself was of an insecure 21-year-old, and her internal image of clean cut 28-year-old Jack was of a delinquent, slightly threatening 19-year-old, wearing black. It wasn't until Gillian's internal image was updated that she was able to truly manage her staff effectively, and reduce the ongoing unexplained pain her osteopath had originally referred her to me for.

Our emotional state has enormous effect on our physiology. At the simplest level, it affects our posture. When you're feeling down, you slump, but when you're feeling great you sit up straight, shoulders back, head up, eyes bright. In fact, the quickest way to change your state if you are feeling down, sleepy or bored is to sit up straight and keep your eyes looking up and out. When we look down we access our memories of feelings, and if they aren't pleasant we spend time wallowing in our pity pit, feeling worse. Slumping also inhibits our ability to breathe efficiently and get enough oxygen to our brain. Sitting up straight at your desk does make a difference. Those teacher nuns were right about one thing, at least!

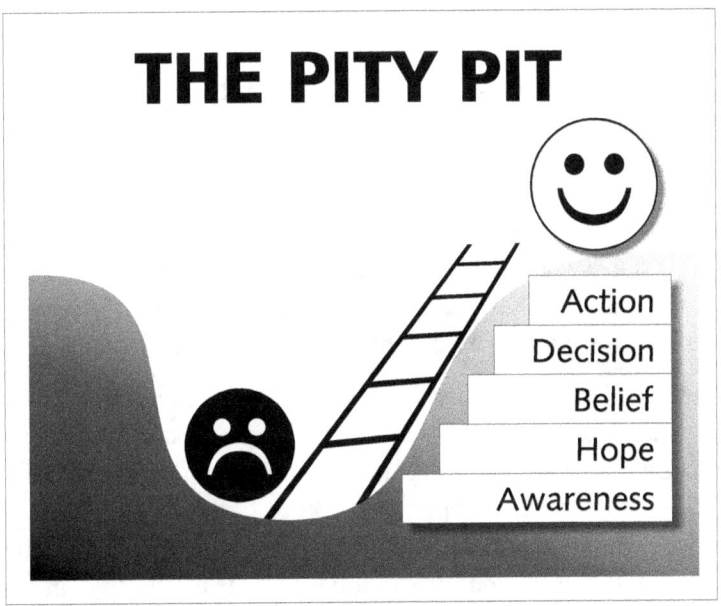

That connection between the emotions and our physiology is where the impact of stress, our ability to maintain a healthy weight to conceive, to create and heal dis-ease is played out. How we feel emotionally and physically determines how we behave, and it's our behaviour that gets us results. The more anger Gillian felt, the more pain she felt in her back, the less tolerant she was with staff, the less responsive her staff became, the more stress Gillian felt, the more she tensed and increased her pain levels ... and so it continued. I'll discuss more about this in Chapter 9, Pain and Dis-Ease.

So if you are experiencing results in your life that you don't like, then we need to go back and check. What are you filtering for? What's happening there that can be changed so we can get a better flow on effect? By changing your focus, you change how you see the world. Change how you feel and then your behaviour changes. Different behaviour gets you into flow that leads to different results. In Chapters 8 to 12, excess weight, unexplained infertility, pain, dis-ease and stress will be discussed in this light.

SIGNIFICANT FILTERS

VALUES

If you ever wondered what your values are, pay attention to how you spend your time, what you think about most, and when you are most happy. Values are simply what is most important to us, so of course they change over time, but their role as motivators cannot be overstated.

Values shift because what was important to you as a five-year-old is different to a 15-year-old, a 25-year-old, and so on. And in a relationship, your values are constantly shifting and changing, so that's why sometimes you're closer together and sometimes you're further apart. That's why friends come into our life and leave again. That's why there can be so much conflict in families, because families don't leave our lives as easily as friends. But absolutely, within the family structure everyone's values are shifting and changing. Whether we share and accept the changes or slip back into old family identity boxes affects on our connection and sense of belonging within the family.

And of course, we can have unconscious values as well. Sometimes what we think is important to us isn't really at the deepest level. For example, we might think that family is important to us but we spend all our time at work. Or we think that health is important, yet we eat where the big golden arches are. When someone on the outside looks at you and says you should be so happy in that job, or that relationship, but if it doesn't feel right inside, that means there's a clash of values for you.

Perhaps you have the high-flying corporate career, your dream car, the luxury goods, but really inside what you really want is to have that baby and stay at home and create a loving, nurturing home environment. Or vice versa. You might have that loving home environment with your children but your heart is screaming, "Give me travel! I want stimulation! I want challenge! I want excitement!".

So, like anything, it's all about finding that balance. As for me, it's not a work-life balance. You don't stop your life when you go to work. It's part of it. You want balance. Life balance. That doesn't mean equal shares either. Ultimately, all anyone really wants is the peace of mind that comes from knowing you are okay, safe, loved, all of your needs and wants are met, and the satisfaction of a life well-lived.

Balance comes from having both golden and power values fulfilled. Golden values are the values we feel good about sharing, such as love, loyalty and health. The power values, for example control and being right, are your true drivers which actually get you out of bed. Once you understand this side of you, they can be harnessed to your goals and speed your progress. Read more about both types of values in Chapter 6.

BELIEFS

In addition to our values filtering all of that information, we've got our beliefs, which include religious and cultural beliefs. But most importantly in this context is self-belief; that is who you believe you are, what you can and can't do, how other people should and shouldn't treat you, whether you are a good person or not, and whether you are lovable or not. All of those beliefs are a significant filter for how you live your life. You can talk yourself into or out of anything, based on your self-beliefs. When did you last say, "Oh I couldn't possibly do that because ..."? How much of your identity is purely based on a belief, perhaps someone else's belief? Watch out for those red flag generalisation words of "always" and "never". What do you hold to be true which is not necessarily so?

MEMORIES

Another filter is memories, and it's an extremely powerful one. For some people, memories are carved in rock, totally non-negotiable; that's how it happened, end of story. The thing with memories is the event no longer exists, except in your mind. By the very nature of memories, what you remember changes depending on how you feel at the time of remembrance. For example, think of an old relationship. Now, if in the present you're feeling loved and happy and strong and confident and you remember; that's totally different from if you're feeling sad and lonely and down and remember. True? That's one reason women go back into dead-end relationships.

Memories don't become a problem except when you use the past as a reason for not moving forward in the present. For example, "I can't save a thing because I failed in maths at Grade Three. It was the teacher's fault. Oh I'd be a success if it wasn't for her. She took all my money". Or maybe, "I'd be able to have a loving relationship if it weren't for my parents' fighting throughout my childhood. He abused me and ruined my life".

If we're feeling down and we remember a negative or a sad event in the past, every time we do that it's almost like adding a grey wash over it. And the more washes we add, the darker and heavier we feel, spiralling down into depression. Learn from the past then take control of your life back. Leave it all behind you where it belongs, and move on. Take responsibility for creating your present and therefore your future.

Speaking of the future, we've also got what I call the "future memories". That's where you go out into the future and do the 'what ifs'. "What if I don't get the job? What if he leaves me? What if I can't? What if I forget what I'm going to say? What if they say no?" All of those negative 'what ifs' keep you where you are. You know those ones!

The problem with the 'what ifs' is that they build up the fear so much it becomes anxiety, that is, a nameless fear. You're afraid and you're not sure of what. Basically, you're afraid of the future. This is hardly surprising because really, if you spend a lot of time picturing all of those negative things out there in the future, who on earth would want to go there? And the future is just a moment away so the fear builds up, into anxiety. While you're imagining out there in the future or back there in the past and you're feeling it, your body doesn't know that it's not real. It feels as if it's really happening. The anger's really happening, the sadness and guilt, whatever it is. But because it's in your head, your body can't run away, and nor can it fight it as your adrenal system is programmed to do. So it just gets stored up in your system and causes you ill health, stress, infertility ... all sorts of issues.

The key is to live in the present. Absolutely have goals and dreams for the future, but live in the present, because in the present you're safe. Right here, right now, you're safe. It's right here, right now that the thoughts you're having, the feelings you're feeling, the actions or inactions, the meaning you give to events, is creating your present, and therefore your future. You will never be wealthy in the future if you don't start creating it now, in the present.

So absolutely, if you catch yourself doing the 'what ifs', the 'should haves', the 'if onlys', bring yourself back to the present. Particularly to counteract the negative 'what ifs'. Asking yourself, "What if it doesn't happen like that?" opens up new possibilities in your mind. Okay, the future may not be that scary, horrible place. It might actually be quite decent. It might even be fun. And then asking yourself, "Well, how would that feel?" and allowing yourself to feel how the opposite would be releases the tension out of your body and at least brings you back to neutral. And if you're really good at imagining the positive 'what ifs', well then you get a buzz out of it, which makes you feel good. You're more likely to take those actions in the present that will get you the future you want.

A word on positive thinking at this point – you don't have to be positive every moment of your day! That's not only hard work, it's downright unrealistic and is setting you up for a low of equal size. Nature prefers equilibrium, so the higher you go, the further you will drop down afterwards. That's why many people who caught up in the high energy frenzy of some personal development seminars get depressed a day or so later. It's nature bringing you back into balance. Now I can hear some of you saying, "Hang on, I don't want my life to be a flat-liner!". Just know that the more you live in your personal power, the more you live your values and purpose, the higher your level of equilibrium, your natural state will be.

Is it likely that the Dalai Lama's equilibrium level is higher than the Average Anna? Of course! Do you think he still experiences anger? Of course! He is human, though the difference is he feels, acknowledges, processes and lets it go much faster than you or I. He doesn't waste energy talking about it, replaying it over and over in his head and projecting a repeat performance in the future. He acknowledged this in response to a journalist's question in a recent television program.

"The present is life's gift to you."

Sue Lester

This point is crucial to your progress, so allow me to reiterate. Right here, right now is the only moment that is real. Everything else, both past and future, exists only in your imagination. So of course you need a vision of your future, of your purpose and how you intend to live a richly fulfilling life, but it is right here, right now in your present that you actually create your future. You create it with your thoughts, your feelings, the meaning you give to events and most of all, you create your future with your actions and inactions in the present.

The more energy you give to imagining all that can go wrong, the less energy you spend in the present creating a richer life, so your negative projections are more likely to manifest through your inactions in the present. Your fears, self-doubts and self-sabotaging thoughts (which I fondly refer to as "The Bitch") will paralyse you, or perhaps send you running, when really you need to stand your ground and fight for all you desire. Isn't it time to ditch *your* bitch?

When you are out there in future, imagining the worst, such is the power of your mind that your body feels it as if it is really happening.

Your body tenses and is flooded with anger, frustration, sadness, fear, hurt or guilt. However, because it is not real, because that scenario only exists in your mind at this point, your body can't action its instinctive flight or fight response. All that angst gets stored in your body, manifesting in tension, headaches, pain, dis-ease, infertility, excess weight and accidents, all signs something is awry in your world. Feeling unwell reduces your energy levels and ability to take creative, decisive action, so it becomes more difficult to produce the results you want, which in turn stresses you more ... and so the downward spiral goes.

Stay present and only visit the future to experience what you do want.

To sum up, there are your values, beliefs and memories filtering the information coming in through all of your senses, creating your reality. This then determines how you feel emotionally and physically, which guides your behaviour, which gives you your results. There are more filters worth mentioning.

DECISIONS

Decisions are all about boundaries and rule books. By 'boundary' I mean the limit of your belief about what you can do, or a block to your progress. Some of us know that whenever we hit a boundary or obstacle we'll find a way under, over, through or around it. Other people hit a boundary in their life and say things like:

"Oh well, that's just how it's mean to be."

"That's just who I am, it can't be helped."

"That's just how our family always does it."

Boundaries or obstacles appearing in your life are actually exciting as they are a sign of progress, a sign you are moving along your life path. They are not a sign (an excuse) to sit down and give up on yourself and your dreams.

The thing with boundaries is that they don't exist, except in your mind. You're never going to walk along the street and come across a big brick wall with a sign saying, "Stop [your name]. This is your boundary."

It's not going to happen, is it? Well, if it does, let me know and I'll write a book about that!

The thing about a boundary is that from the inside you need to be able to push it out as far as you need to. Of course, we're always braver in some areas of our lives than others. I know someone who is incredibly wealthy and is extremely brave in business and wealth creation but his boundary when it comes to personal relationships is really close to his body because he just doesn't do it well. Asking an attractive woman, any woman actually, out on a date turns him to jelly. He doesn't see himself as attractive or desirable, and doesn't have the self-love to allow someone else to love him. I would so love the opportunity to help him to let go and grow.

So, you're pushing the boundary out as far as you need to go from the inside. But from the outside, to other people, your boundaries do need to be brick walls, otherwise you end up spending your life fulfilling other people's needs and expectations of your life, rather than yours. You've seen that with toddlers, haven't you? If you haven't had a child yourself, you've seen them in supermarkets when they're told "No"; they keep asking and asking and asking until Mum or Dad gives in. They're just pushing the boundaries until they get what they want. What you're teaching them is just to keep pushing. Tenacity in business is powerful, but not good for household harmony.

Therefore it's important that when you set a boundary you maintain it. Or if you're going to change your mind, do it straight away under negotiation. It makes it easier for everyone.

THE 'TWO NO RULE'

I favour the Two No Rule which I started using after visiting Nepal the first time. The Nepali shopkeepers would have a price on an item, and if you asked politely there was often a lower second price. There it stopped. There was no outrageous first price and endless bargaining down to the last coin, as in India and Tanzania. In my Two No Rule, the second no is absolute. That gives the child a chance to plead their case and you the opportunity to reconsider your initial "No". Children as young as four can be taught this rule. Consistency is the key to success, as it often is in parenting, in business and in life.

A warning if you're putting up boundaries and saying "No" to people where as in the past you've always said "Yes", even at your own expense. Just know that they will be banging their heads against that new boundary. And also know that some people are really, really slow learners, so it's going to take them a while, and some pain, to stop banging their head against your wall. It's kinder for you and them for you to maintain that boundary because if you let them bang their heads quite a few times and then let the wall drop they get hurt and confused, rather than learn the lesson. You feel guilty and the whole thing becomes a big mess, with you firmly in the middle. You may have experienced this before.

Effective boundary setting and maintenance is a crucial part of your personal growth. If you haven't been maintaining your boundaries, you may just spend your whole life fulfilling other people's needs and values, and not your own. It's not about being selfish. Whether you're a mother, a daughter, a cousin, a son, a husband, whatever, if you don't set boundaries and fulfil your own needs, fill up your own well, then you've nothing to give people. You let them take and take and take until your well is almost dry. You know what's at the bottom of an empty well, don't you? There's mud, there's slime, and dead things (your dreams perhaps?). Not much good for you, let alone anyone else. So fill up your own well first so you can overflow and give people more, at home and at work.

Sometimes, saying "No" is the very best thing you can do for someone, because then they need to stand on their own two feet and find their own solutions and action. They need to step up and take responsibility for their own lives, no matter what age they are. If you are caught in the rescue cycle with your adult children, check what unconscious blueprint™ images you have of them. If you still hold an image of your son as a child then you will not be able to allow him to truly be a man in your presence. Ensure you have recent photos on display in your home. Remove those cute baby pictures from your wallet.

My oldest client to date was 76 and she actually came to me because she was tired of her older sister bullying her. She decided enough was enough. I really admire her for pushing her boundary out at that age, but I would hope that you don't wait that long. Take action now because your life is not tomorrow, it's right now. Tomorrow may never come.

> *"Sometimes the very best way to help someone is to say no to them."*
>
> Sue Lester

LANGUAGE

Language is a very powerful filter, because we create our reality through our perceptions of events. In other words, we talk to ourselves about what is happening and can empower or disempower ourselves with our self-talk. In addition, we have a language filter which may block out a third or two-thirds of the conversation we are participating in. There are three different language styles determined by the individual's lead representational system; visual, auditory and kinaesthetic. For example, some people are more visual, "I see what you mean. Let me paint you a picture of how it'll look". Others are more auditory, "I hear what you're saying. That rings a bell". Kinaesthetic people may say, "I get what you mean. I feel for you. I get goose bumps thinking about it". The predicates people use in speech are indicators of their preferred language style, and by responding in kind you'll more easily build rapport. Powerful communicators naturally or intentionally use a combination of all three. Which style do you use most often? And your partner? Children? Colleagues? Play with speaking in their language and notice the difference.

The most potent way language filters is in the power of self-talk. In the thousands of thoughts we have each day, research shows 95 per cent are exactly the same as the day before. Are you talking yourself into success or failure? Commonly, the most savage critic in someone's life is the one that sits on your shoulder and tells you nasty stories about your failures in the past, what people really think of you, and what a mess you're going to make of the future, no matter how hard to you try. That voice (The Bitch) will tell you your flaws and weaknesses, generalising wildly and widely about your ability in any given situation.

The thing is that the voice isn't even necessarily yours. If you listen carefully, you might hear the words from way back when. Someone who was important in your life, back in your childhood perhaps, said something and at the time you believed it with every little fibre of your body. Since then, you've been repeating it to yourself until it now sounds like your voice, your identity. It's not, unless you choose it to be, and unconsciously construct an internal blueprint to match.

We say things to ourselves that we would never accept from anyone else in our life. So next time you catch yourself feeling critical, tense or unhappy, just notice what you're saying to yourself. That you'll never be able to do it, that you're a loser and you've failed again, you're not lovable, you're too fat, you're too this, you're not enough that. Just check in because that self-talk is actually programming you. Importantly, it's either programming you for success and happiness or it's programming you for failure and misery. Along with failure and misery comes pain and ill-health. It's your choice, and that's where your personal power comes in. You take responsibility for making the changes that you want to see in your life. You're not expected to do it all by yourself, so relax.

Okay, so basically the two million bits deleted, distorted and generalised through all your filters determines your focus, what your R.A.S. highlights. What you focus on is what you get, so make sure you focus on what you do want rather than what you don't want. What you focus on determines how you see the world so if you're focussing on poverty or lack, then that's what you're going to notice in your world. If you're focussing on the statement, "I don't want to be fat" then you're going to notice all of those takeaway foods or the fatty options as your unconscious doesn't process the "don't", just the "fat". (Remember the 'don't think of a green dog' pre-reading exercise?) If you're focussing on good health and a healthy body, you'll notice the fruit and the salads, the stairs rather than the escalators.

Have you ever gone into a restaurant and looked at the menu or at the display cabinet and made your choice, and then someone beside you chooses something you didn't even see, that you didn't know existed? It just wasn't on your radar.

And that's the key. By adjusting your filters you can change your area of focus. It's like being able to shine a torch on a different area. Because remember, there are two million bits per second knocking on your senses, and just because you're only absorbing 126 of them, it doesn't mean the rest don't exist. People who seem more successful than you are simply noticing and taking action on a different 126 bits. So by adjusting your filters we enable you to actually access different options, resources, people, and alternative ways of behaving.

That can be quite empowering, yet for some people it can be absolutely terrifying because what do you do if you can't blame someone else? What if it's up to you? You have to take responsibility. Deep down you already know that if your life isn't the way you want it, the only person that can change it is you. If you didn't, you wouldn't have even noticed this book, let alone be reading it. That's part of working through and growing and evolving; accepting that, yes, I am responsible for my own thoughts, feelings, actions or inactions, and the meaning I give to events. That is all part of stepping into your personal power. Are you ready to reclaim your personal power? Great, so let's continue on to Chapter 5.

TIME TO CHANGE EXERCISE

If you write down anything today, write these questions down where you can re-read them as needed. "What if it doesn't? How would that feel?" And then every time you catch yourself having that negative thought, ask yourself those two questions and notice how different you feel.

KEY POINTS

- Everyone has a different reality, based on how they filter the information flooding their senses.
- It's the meaning you give to an event, not the event itself, that makes the difference.
- Expecting others to filter information exactly the same way as you sets you up for hurt.
- Question: How can he do / say that? Answer: Because he is not me.
- Values and memories are two of the strongest filters which create your reality.
- The past and future only exist in your imagination. The only real moment is the present.
- Anxiety control: "What if it doesn't happen like that? How will that feel?"
- You can learn to control your imagination, therefore your past, present and future.
- Positive thinking 100 per cent of the time is unrealistic, and trying is depressing.
- The Two No Rule helps with setting new boundaries, and disciplining children.
- Language is what we use to explain what we experience to ourselves and others. It creates our individual realities.

BONUS: Go to www.growingcontent.com.au and sign up to my monthly newsletter to get your free copy of my e-book, Win-Win Loving: Your Guide To Even More Loving Relationships and Harmonious Homes.

*"You learnt to walk without worrying about what other people might think about your efforts. Trying and not succeeding is not failure.
Failure is not even trying, because 'What if ...?'"*

Sue Lester

FIVE.

RECLAIMING YOUR PERSONAL POWER INCLUDING FINANCIAL FREEDOM

So, what is personal power? Personal power, for me, is not about huge egos or bullying. Take a moment to consider this and no doubt you'll think of people in your life who have got it. They're the ones who are calm, confident, centred. They know who they are. They like who they are. They generally have a clear sense of direction, where they're heading in their life. They might not be able to see every single step on the path, because who can? Some people have 30 or 80-year plans, plans that go well past their own life span, mapping out the legacy they will leave from living their purpose. They have faith in their ability to find whatever they need to get there: the creativity, ideas, people, education, coaches, mentors, support team around them, personally and in business, plus whatever other resources are needed.

Have you considered what your legacy will be? Is it raising your children to be the adults the world needs to thrive? Is it your book? Perhaps it's the economic impact of your successful business? Is it the effect of your kind words and deeds each day? That bright idea you made real?

My tangled life path didn't result in children, so I was at a loss as to what my legacy would be, until I worked out what my purpose is. My purpose is to be a catalyst of change, travelling the world, writing, speaking and helping people let go and grow. For every person I help to clear head trash and step into their personal power, there is a positive ripple effect throughout their whole life, to their spouse, children, family, friends, colleagues, clients, employees and out in the community, for generations to come.

For you know when you are unhappy and unfulfilled, sacrificing yourself for others as you've been taught, your loved ones suffer. Your children cop your frustrations, miss out on a better role model, and go on to parent their children as you do. Your unhappy spouse performs at less than his peak at work, which eventually impacts on the company's bottom line, and ultimately the economy. You don't notice someone else's pain so don't reach out to heal. Unhappy homes and workplaces are unhealthy places, so you suffer more from ills and pains. And worst of all, you don't fulfil your own purpose on earth. What will your legacy be? Are you ready now to put the "I" back into your life?

People who have tapped into their personal power know their legacy, plus have a sense of fun, enthusiasm and passion. Living in your personal power you are calm, confident, centred, you know who you are, like who you are, know where you're heading and have faith in your ability to get there.

The diagram below illustrates the components of stepping into your personal power, and the opposite end of the continuum.

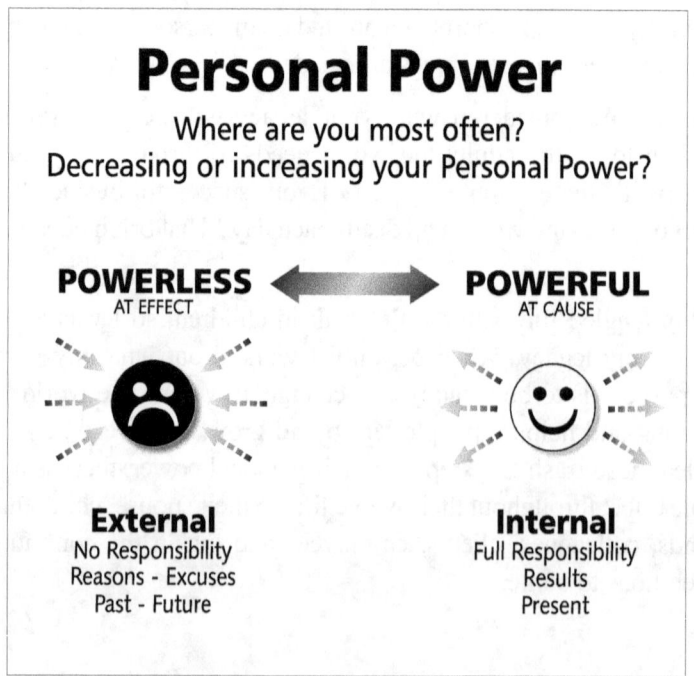

POWERLESS / AT EFFECT

Let's examine the 'Powerless', the 'At Effect' side of the continuum first. The sad face with the arrows pointing in represents that it's a miserable place to be, for most people, because the world is happening to you. You have no control and are buffeted by life's events.

EXTERNAL / EXCUSES

The Powerless perspective sees the external world (government, weather, world economy and other people) as in power, so the battles are fought externally. Ultimately, this means no responsibility needs to be taken as it's not your fault, it's theirs, those external forces. It is always someone else's fault when you don't achieve your desired results. People at this end are quick with reasons and excuses why it is so. They point to the past for blame, and highlight the 'should haves' and the 'if onlys'.

NO RESPONSIBILITY

I say most people find it a miserable place, because I have, as possibly you have, encountered people who thrive on living their lives At Effect. They are the ones who seem to generate dramas in their lives for excitement and meaning, and / or willingly rort our social security system as if the world owes them a living. And in their reality it does, which is why for some there is no motivation to change. It's perfectly understandable that their children grow up with the same values.

A former neighbour was a classic case study in this. She complained bitterly she only had a three-bedroom house supplied by the government. However, as most of her children were in foster care, three bedrooms were deemed enough. Her screaming matches with her 14-year-old daughter would start in the house, move into the front garden, and continue down the street, fading off into the distance, then getting louder and louder as they came back up the street to their house. Fascinating. It was so quiet after her violently abusive boyfriend burnt the house down. I heard she then was granted a four-bedroom house as she was pregnant again, and they moved in together.

BLAMING THE PAST

A client once said to me, "If it weren't for my Grade Three teacher I'd be really good at maths, and if I were really good at maths, I'd be able to save and manage my money and I wouldn't have maxed out my credit card. So, it's all her fault. She was such a mean cow". Others point the finger at their parents or former spouses and say, "If it weren't for him, I'd be a success now". Imagine how very different Oprah's life would be today if she'd lived her life At Effect. She'd still be in abject poverty, abused and blaming her gender and skin colour!

That reminds me of an interesting study on identical twins done in the United States which I've heard about from various sources over the years. There was one set the researchers were particularly interested in because these boys ended up on different ends of the economic spectrum. One was living on the streets, and one had forged a life as an extremely successful businessman. They both grew up in the same house with an emotionally and physically abusive father. The researchers asked each of the twins the same question: "How do you explain where you ended up?" And each twin said exactly the same thing, "With a father like mine, how could I not?"

BLAMING THE FUTURE

While some choose to blame the past, others will point at the future as a reason not to change. They say, "I'd do that but what if she doesn't like it? I'd take this job but what if it doesn't work out? What if I'm not good enough? I can't do that investment because what if? What if? What if? What if?" The 'what ifs' become a block for moving forward and growing and evolving. "I'm 40. I'm too old to study now. I'd be 44 when I finished or 48 if I do it part-time." And your point? All going well you're going to be 48 someday anyway. It's just a difference between whether you're going to have a degree or regrets.

Being At Effect is very much stuck with the 'should haves,' or the 'if onlys' and the 'what ifs,' and using that as a reason not to move forwards.

So At Effect is very much about excuses and reasons. Why you can't do this. All the reasons why your life isn't everything you ever wanted it to be. You give your personal power away by forgetting you have choices, saying:

"I don't have time."

"I'm too tired."

"I have to look after the children."

"I would but my husband needs to go to soccer."

"I know I should be studying or listening to that audio but I'm addicted to *Master Chef*."

You know if something tremendously exciting or life threatening came up, you could find the time and energy to prioritise it, true?

INACTION

Living At Effect is also very much about inaction. Nothing's happening and you're stuck. You may be comfy in your little rut (habits) or on the comfy couch, as some people call it, but nothing much is happening. Every year you have your anniversary and nothing much has changed. As far as you look forward, nothing much is changing. Some people find security in that, and other people just get more and more depressed. Being At Effect is very much being the victim. You can't take action because you're too disempowered and you're too disempowered because you've got no responsibility. It's all external. It's all about 'them'. It's their fault entirely, not yours.

CONTINUUM

So, it's not a pleasant place to be full-time, and some people spend their lives very much At Effect. No doubt you know people who are in that situation. However, the majority of people are somewhere along the continuum in any area of their life at any given point of time in their day.

I've never encountered anyone who lives 100 per cent in their personal power in every area of their life every moment of every day. We are human, and that's what makes life stimulating. The key is to be aware of your power, and to make choices that have you living At Cause for the majority of time. If you notice you are disempowering yourself, give yourself a pat on the back for noticing, and ask yourself how you'd prefer to be feeling / thinking / acting. The 3 Steps To Healing in Chapter 6 is a great tool to help with this.

> *"You weren't born asking, 'Does my bum look in this nappy?'"*
>
> Sue Lester

POWERFUL / AT CAUSE

INTERNAL

Let's examine the 'Powerful' (At Cause) side of the continuum. The smiley face with the arrows radiating out indicates you're happening to the world, and you understand your power is internal. Your strength comes from within. When a decision is to be made, you check in with your own values and take action based on that because you trust your own ability to do so. When you are buffeted by life's challenges, just like everyone else, there is a deep inner core, a knowing that you're okay. You're worthy, you're enough, and yes, you will make it home.

FULL RESPONSIBILITY

Knowing your personal power source is internal enables you to take full responsibility for your life and everything that's in it. Your life is a reflection of choices you've made since you came into conscious awareness. For example, your health is a direct result of how you've chosen to treat your body, in terms of its fuel, maintenance, rest, exercise, your self-talk (increasing stress levels), exposure to high risk environments (public transport during a flu epidemic, working conditions, chemicals), and your response when you do get caught by a passing bug. Do you soldier on regardless of your body's protests? I'll explore the mind-body connection more in Chapters 8 to 10.

The key is that we can't control every life event, but we do have a choice about how we respond to that event. You're taking full responsibility for your own thoughts. You take full responsibility for your own feelings, for your own actions or inactions. "Wasn't me. I didn't do it." Yes, that's the point. You didn't do anything when you could have stepped up and made a difference. And full responsibility, most importantly, for the meaning you give to events in your life. An important note here, you are not taking responsibility for other people's stuff, just your own. You're not responsible for people choosing to be angry or choosing to feel guilty or hurt or whatever it is. I'll come back to that significant distinction soon.

MEANING

For the moment, back to the importance of the meaning we give to happenings in our lives. Take the twin study example. For one, having a violent, abusive father meant that he was worthless because he believed everything his father said. Therefore, the choices he made in his life lead him to end up living on the streets. The other twin responded differently. He refused to believe the things his father said to him. He took all that abuse to mean that he just needed to get out of home as quickly as possible. He decided the most effective way of doing that was to get a job, make loads of money, thrive, and prove that mongrel wrong. So the meaning he gave to his father's abuse was actually his impetus to go on and achieve.

The same applies to the example of my client blaming a maths teacher for her maxed out credit card. Two students fail a maths test. For one, it means she's useless at maths, useless at finances, and will never be able to manage money. The other just thinks, "Well, hang on, I should have studied more. Maybe I shouldn't have gone out with my friends last night? Maybe I should have asked more questions or got a tutor if I didn't understand the way the teacher taught? So what if I don't like him? It's my learning that's important, whether he's a good teacher or not."

Admittedly, many eight-year-olds don't necessarily have that reasoning capacity, but by adulthood we do. We retain the capacity to learn throughout our whole life. The only constant thing in our busy modern lives is change, so if we didn't have the capacity to learn we could not function. Adults trip themselves up on the expectation that they will get a new skill or concept 100 per cent right in the first attempt – without having to actually learn through experimentation and practice.

Here is another quite common example of the impact of meaning you give to events. Imagine walking along the street bumping into someone you haven't seen for ages. When you greet her she's not as friendly or welcoming as you would expect. You could take that to mean, "She's a snobby cow", or, "They've been talking about me behind my back again", or, 'I'm not good enough to be her friend". You could imagine all sorts of meanings which disempower, so you respond with guarded body language and tone, and you're not particularly warm because of your own insecurities.

But what if she has a headache? What if her cat died that morning? What if she's just feeling down? All she needed was a little understanding kindness to lift her up, and your insecurities denied her that. You both leave feeling uncomfortable, and next time you met there's already a barrier to rapport. Particularly if you've both spent time creating stories in your head and sharing them with others about the situation.

So you can see how easily miscommunication happens in the world. We put meaning on other people's behaviour, impacting on our own behaviour. They interpret that a different way and it just becomes messier and messier and messier. Perhaps you've experienced this at family gatherings or in the workplace? Think of that event, and knowing what you know now, how will you respond differently in the future?

RESPONSIBILITY FOR YOURS ONLY

I highlighted earlier that being in your personal power, At Cause, means taking full responsibility for your own stuff, but not anyone else's. Imagine giving unsolicited advice to a colleague, and she responds by yelling at you and is now ignoring you, even though you work on the same team.

You take full responsibility for giving unsolicited advice, for your intention, timing, words, tone, body language, clarity of meaning of the message, method and place of delivery, the potential disruption to your team's productivity, and how you've behaved since the event. You don't take responsibility for how she chose to respond and her ongoing behaviour. She could choose to to yell, burst into tears, calmly tell you to mind your own business, laugh or dismiss your opinion with a polite, "I appreciate your concern". She has a choice about how she behaved subsequently, choosing to resolve the issues or continue the awkward situation, as do you.

Taking responsibility for other people's stuff will tie you up in knots of fear and guilt, unable to move because 'what if' they don't approve, get angry or stop liking you? Just as you don't like everyone in the world and how they choose to live their lives, not everyone in the world will like you and how you choose to live your life. That's perfectly okay, and as long as you are living in your personal power, it will also feel okay.

PRESENT

Living in your personal power is very much about being in the present. Remember, At Effect you're in the past with the 'should-haves', the 'if onlys' and out in the future with the 'what ifs'. At Cause, where your personal power lies, is very much in the present because it's only the present that is real. The rest exists in your past and future memory. It's only in the present that you can actually create your future by taking action in thought, speech or deed. Here is where the magic happens.

In the present is where the fun is! How many of us are actually living our lives two steps ahead of where we are, and missing all the fun? You may have already noticed this, but if not, next time you go to a cafe or restaurant, just have a look around. At how many tables are people sitting there – with friends presumably – and they're actually on their mobile, talking to someone else, or playing with apps? I especially noticed this on New Year's Eve, when you see it all the time in huge groups. Lots of people spending so much time telling others who are somewhere else how much fun they're having that they're not actually having fun. It's just all these isolated people on their phones, which is a bit sad, really. All of those moments of connection, of relationship building, wasted.

RESULTS

At Effect was about excuses and reasons. At Cause, where your personal power is, is focussed on results. You'll always get results. It is a matter of whether you like them or not. Rather than label undesirable results as mistakes and failures and beat yourself up with a big stick and nasty names, you have a choice. You could calmly accept it as results you didn't want, and ask yourself, "Well, what do I need to modify to get the results I want?" By doing that, by actively seeking alternatives, you actually feel more empowered, and far more likely to ultimately get those results you want.

Ideal results at the first attempt are ideal, not necessarily realistic, particularly if it is a new venture and you're stretching your boundaries. Allow yourself to learn and accept that it is what it is, not a character flaw or identity crisis on your part. We'd be still living in caves if Urg had given up the first time he tried to make fire and didn't get the results he wanted. And if you know a successful person who has never had results he or she didn't want, please email me as I'd love to interview him or her.

Remember that time you had that experience which didn't work out so well, but you've thought, "Okay, I can do this better next time". And when you do it, you get different results and doesn't it feel so much better? Rather than being a victim, over there At Effect you're the victor. It's not about being brave all the time or being courageous and superior. Courage is feeling the fear and doing it anyway. Stepping out of our comfort zones and pushing ourselves is when personal growth and fulfilment happen. Once you've pushed and achieved, no matter how small, acknowledge that you've made progress. And even if you don't get the results you want – because, of course, we always get results – at least you've taken action, and any movement is movement forwards. Once you're moving, you can change direction. It's much easier to change direction once you're moving, rather than when you're stuck. You'll know this to be true if you've ever tried to push a car, or watched someone else do it.

 TIME TO CHANGE EXERCISE: PERSONAL POWER AND FINANCES

So, how can you apply all this? How can you get personal power into your life? Here is an exercise to help. You'll need a piece of paper and a pen.

On a fresh page, divide it in half and label the left had side At Effect and the right hand side At Cause. Once you've done that, think of an area in your life where you're not getting the results you want. You could also use this for a specific problem you want to dissect. As you think about all the ways that issue is a problem for you, write your thoughts about it on the left hand side under At Effect.

For example, your list might be something like:

FINANCES	
AT EFFECT	AT CAUSE
I don't have enough money.	
I don't get paid enough.	
My credit card is almost maxed out.	
I'm fighting with my partner.	
I can't buy the clothes I really want.	
It's always a struggle.	
I can't see it getting any better.	
He's spending too much money.	

Write them all down on the left hand side, as many as you need to get out of your system.

And just a point here, if you ever catch yourself blaming someone else, blaming them for you not moving forward or for how you feel, just know that's very much At Effect. You are effectively giving your personal power to that person by giving them control over the happiness in your day, the success in your life. As Eleanor Roosevelt said, "No one can make you feel inferior without your permission".

During a workshop I had a participant strongly object to that quote. She said it really annoyed her as it was all right for confident people, but what about people like her who weren't born that way? Interestingly, it took confidence for her to speak up in a group setting. She was limiting herself by the stories she was telling herself about her abilities.

Personally, even though I was a school teacher, I used to struggle with public speaking. Eventually I invested in training that cleared my fears as well as teaching me speaking and platform skills. I stopped telling myself I was nervous, inexperienced, stopped wondering what the audience might say about my height or hairdo, and stopped imagining myself failing. I now do the reverse, and it's so much easier, so much fun to grow my business by sharing what I love by speaking to many.

> *"The only difference between confident and not confident people is the story they tell themselves. Are you empowering or disempowering yourself?"*
>
> *Sue Lester*

Let me give you another example. Just say you're in a work situation. You put in a lot of effort and the project didn't come out the way it was meant to because the other person didn't work as hard as you. Your share of the responsibility of that result includes not monitoring it more closely and not putting an alternative strategy into place when you realised he wasn't actually doing his share.

I'd like to get back to the finance exercise, and how you can use your personal power to build your financial control. So, on your left hand side you've got your area, your problem. Dump it all down. And you'll notice I put it on the left rather than a combination of left and right because generally when we're feeling bad about something we tend to be At Effect. You'll find most things you're struggling with actually belong on the left hand side. True?

Part of making that deep level shift and getting that financial control is taking that responsibility – full responsibility – for your thoughts, feelings and actions. "I don't have enough money" is a huge disempowering generalisation which feels emotionally heavy. That heaviness keeps you inert. Part of being in control is being specific. Cut that generalisation into manageable chunks, and it will be much easier to find solutions, then take action.

So, you don't have enough money? For what, specifically? Are your basics – your food, shelter, and utilities – covered? If not, then your first action step is to make a phone call today to book in to see a professional financial counsellor this week (at Lifeline, for example). A painfully embarrassing process, yes, but the sooner you seek professional help the better. Seriously, if you're not covering your basics, you need help, now, while it's just raining. Don't wait for the flood. Perhaps you really meant, "I don't have enough money to dine out every week / to have an overseas holiday / to replace my old car / to feel secure with a cash buffer".

Personal power is about changing your focus to increase your personal power. So, have a look at each of those items in turn – the ones you wrote on the left. Make them more specific, then consider.

How can you actually step into your personal power and take responsibility and therefore action, on each one of those? For example, "I don't get paid enough". For what, specifically? For the hours you work or to afford that sexy car? Then consider what can you do? Write those answers in the right hand column. For example, get a new, better paid job. (Note: 'better paid' rather than just 'new'.) Sometimes what you are wanting is already in front of you. Ask for a raise. Ask for that promotion. Ask to be moved to a different department with more opportunities. But of course, it's not just a matter of asking. You need to be prepared for this. It's critical you do your homework, be really clear why you're worth it. So you can go on holidays is not a good enough reason. (I know, bosses can be unreasonable like that sometimes!) Be clear about what you want, why you are worth it, and how that benefits the company, in terms of a raise or promotion.

What else can you do? Do you need a second job? If you are a business owner, shift your focus and start paying yourself first. Be clear about what you want, why you are worth it, and how that benefits the company in terms of a raise or promotion (sound familiar?).

What else could you do?

Also consider these questions in relation to "I don't get paid enough". Is it that I'm not getting paid enough for what I want to buy, or is that I'm not managing my money? Do I need to save and have a savings plan I actually commit to, even if it's only a small amount each pay? As Dr John Demartini teaches, it's not the amount you save; it's the habit of saving that makes the difference.

Consider Jason and Jackie. Jason scoffs at Jackie's commitment to save $20 per pay, and decides $500 will reach his target faster, even though he isn't currently saving anything. He struggles to put any money aside, and each pay he tells himself he'll put in more next time to make it up. He saved $500 out of his tax return then withdrew it for his holiday spending money, so ends up at the end of the year in the same savings-less situation. Jackie's automatic savings plan worked so well she became excited with her success, and started pushing her boundaries, increasing her savings deduction a little more every couple of months, until at the end of the year she had saved $2,640. She then reinvested in a higher interest bearing account. It's not the amount; it's the habit of saving that makes the difference.

Let's look at another example, "My credit card's almost maxed out". Taking full responsibility and stepping into your personal power, ask, "How do I take responsibility and therefore action on that point?". Some possible answers are: firstly, stop using it. Cut it up. If you're paying 20 per cent interest, that means for every $1,000 you're actually paying an extra $200. That item actually cost $1,200 not $1,000. Ouch – not such a bargain after all. Only spend the money you actually have. And pay it off regularly, even a little bit is better than nothing. Reduce the limit as you go and then when you've paid it off, close it down and replace it with a debit card. That way you only spend money you have. Remember, you are saying no from love, not to punish yourself.

Yes, I know there are ways you can get points, leverage off other people's money, and use credit cards as powerful tools. Absolutely. Credit cards aren't evil, they are simply a tool which can be used to create or destroy. Be clear, if your credit card is maxed out and you can't pay it off completely each month so you avoid paying interest, that's not the method for you.

Next example: what if on your list was fighting with your partner about money issues? Be specific about why you're fighting. Is it about your spending or is it about his spending? Is it that you don't value what you are both spending money on? Are you fighting because you feel that he's not earning enough? Are you punishing him? Is it really about sex? Are you unhappy because when you were little you dreamed that you would have a wonderful life and the reality isn't matching up to that? Every time you see your partner, it's a reminder that you're not living your dream, that he's not a rich Prince Charming, just a man?

So, how can you take responsibility and therefore action, to shift things around? Because, while you're getting your finances under control, the last thing you need is fighting and discord in your daily life. You want to feel good about your life and feel loving towards the person you've chosen to share it with. So he's not a prince, but you aren't a princess, are you?

Remember that the next time you snarl at your spouse, it is your choice to be with that person. Yes, there are consequences for leaving as there are for staying, but regardless, unless he keeps you under lock and key, it is ultimately your life, your choice. Consider all aspects of your options, listen to your intuition, make your choice, and commit to making it your best choice. More about this in Chapter 7, Putting The I Back into Your LIFE, and Chapter 11, Relationships Refreshed.

If one of the things on your list is that you have too many bills, and "I hate paying bills", take a step outside of that for a moment. Many bills we pay are for essential services, for example, electricity, telephone, water, our home (mortgage / rent), roads and sewerage etcetera. Actually, we've been given credit for up to three months for services we've already used. Imagine if it was a 'pay-as-you-go' system – how much more difficult would daily life be then?

Start putting money aside each pay for those regular bills (yes, you've heard that before, but are you actually doing it?). Next month the angst won't be there if you've already got the money set aside, and you feel grateful you've had unfettered access to that service already. Your payment is simply a thank you to the service provider. Just as you expect your clients or your employer to pay you without rancour, keep that money flowing around with gratitude. If you've travelled overseas or seen the homeless in your town, or even watched TV, you'll know there are millions who would love to have your 'problem'. There are millions who would love to live your 'worst' day in preference to theirs.

Living in your personal power is about perspective and taking responsibility for what you can change, and at the very least, that is always your attitude.

Some of my travel memories have just come to mind which may help add a different perspective for you.

Bouncing in the back of a truck sliding along a mud track through a village in the Republic of Congo, I noticed the village's sole source of income was a large bunch of green bananas and a bag of charcoal. I suddenly realised my backpack, housing my few clothes and sleeping bag, cost more than the whole village's annual income.

Sitting by the side of the road in Malawi, chatting with a local as we waited in vain for a lift up to the Zomba Plateau, him asking what our staple food in Australia was, for example maize or rice? How could I even begin to explain the extent of choice in our supermarkets, takeaway shops, cafes and restaurants? Confess to the billion dollar weight loss industry?

Dodging huge potholes in roads near Goroka in PNG that could have been repaired, had not the money disappeared into corrupt official pockets. Being grateful next time I paid my car registration, and was delayed by road works in progress.

In Ladakh in northern India, sitting in a nomad's woven yak hair summer tent, trying to explain why we came all the way from Australia to walk in her backyard mountains. She asked what we had paid and said, "Next time you come walk with me!", feeling her pity for me as I had no children, so in her eyes, no real wealth.

In the Annapurna region of Nepal, visiting a bare cement slab school with no electricity where students from far away villages boarded in huts they built themselves: simple plank beds, pitch black with no windows, and dank water pooled on the floor.

Walking into my home after a month spent walking across the Australian Simpson Desert, nomadic style with camels, sleeping in a swag, cooking over open fires, with rationed water for drinking and cooking only. (That first shower in Birdsville at the end was orgasmic.) I looked around my house and wondered why I had ever thought I needed all that stuff.

The more you do this exercise, writing things down, shifting your focus, taking responsibility and therefore action, the less overwhelming anxiety you feel because a sense of control comes from taking action. You're being specific about the issue. You're not making huge, disempowering generalisations about not having or being enough. Once you're specific, it becomes manageable. Once you've got that awareness you can actually take action and make those changes you want to have.

It's a beautifully simple process, and in the words of one of my Personal Power Transformation program participants, " ... it seems like the moment you sit down and write this out – a situation that you dislike or want to change – it instantly gives you an emotion of self-power". It works because it's about awareness and specific action, rather than blaming someone else and saying, "Well I can't do anything. It's not my fault". Taking action, even if you don't instantly get your ultimate results, increases your self-esteem.

Take a moment to think of examples in your own past. The times where you do step up, you do feel better about yourself, don't you? You feel less helpless, more in control. And if you have children, friends, family, you become a role model for them. That feels satisfying too.

Self-awareness is about observing without judgement or self-consciousness. The better you understand yourself and what truly drives you, the better choices you can make for yourself. Next chapter is all about discovering your power values, your true motivators, so get ready for a walk on your dark side!

KEY POINTS

» **Living in your personal power** you are calm, confident, centred, you know who you are, you like who you are, you know where you're heading, and have faith in your ability to get there.

» **Living At Effect** you are playing the victim, giving your responsibility and therefore power away by blaming others, the past and the future. Focussing on excuses not results, staying stuck. Telling yourself you can't help eating chocolate biscuits instead of fruit, when all you need to do is stop buying the biscuits.

» **Living At Cause** you are powerful, taking full responsibility for your own actions, meaning and emotional state, and the results produced. You live in the present where you can create the future you desire

*"How you act shouts so loudly
I can't hear what you are saying."*

Unknown

SIX.
POWER VALUES: YOUR TRUE DRIVERS

The basis of what I call 'power values' comes from the personal coaching I did with Benjamin J. Harvey when he was initially developing his Shadow Values concept and processes. For more on Shadow Values visit www.authenticeducation.com.au.

In this chapter we examine what values are, their importance in creating change in our lives, plus the significance of power values and how to harness them to speed your progress.

VALUES

First of all, what are values? Basically, your values are simply what is important to you. They are another filter you use to help process all the information coming in through your senses. Obviously, you'll be on alert and notice what's important to you. Your R.A.S. (Reticular Activating System) will be programmed to allow in relevant stimulus. For example, walking along a street I may notice a car if it was in my favourite red, or a particularly loud or offensive colour, but otherwise it would be off my radar. On the other hand, cars are of interest, therefore value, to my partner, so he not only notices cars, he can tell me the make, model and approximate year of the cars too. He'll spend time reading about cars. I won't, unless I'm intending to buy one, in which case certain cars become important to me, and I'll notice them driving past and in the media.

The key point here is that if you want more of something in your life, whether money, sex, love, business success or glowing health, you need to move it up your values list so it becomes higher on your radar, so to speak. There is a variety of NLP techniques to do this quickly, but you can also make a conscious decision to commit to change. You then must allocate time to focus on your new value. For example, if you want wealth to be your highest value, you need to spend more time on wealth than anything else. You fill your waking hours reading, researching, talking, thinking and learning everything to do with creating, growing and retaining (very important!) wealth. This is where agreed shared values with your spouse become critical to the success of your relationship. It's also crucial to be crystal clear on who you are and what you genuinely want in your life. Wealth at the expense of family and loving relationships is not an ideal outcome for many people.

Of course, our values change over time naturally. Just think, what's important to you as a five-year-old is different to you as a 15-year-old, a 25-year-old, and so on. Most of us are aware of some of our values. If I asked what's important to you, you would probably tell me things like love, family, wealth, freedom, loyalty, trust, adventure, education and security. They're all what I call our golden values, our lighter side. They're the sort of things you wouldn't mind sharing with people in public.

Take a moment now to think about and write down your top values. There's no wrong answer, so write down what comes to mind, even if it surprises you.

_____
_____
_____
_____
_____
_____
_____

But, of course, you know that in life there is always balance. So where there's light, there is also dark. On one side of the values coin are golden values and on the flip side is what I call our power values. Imagine, for a moment, you're lying in bed in the morning and it's time to get up. If you know your golden values are going to be fulfilled, that is, you're going to feel loved, you're going to have that sense of freedom of choice, you're going to connect with those around you and you're going do to something adventurous, well it would make it really easy to get out of bed, wouldn't it?

If, on the other hand, you're lying there in bed and you know that you're absolutely not going to be feeling the love today, it's going to be just a boring drag, you're going to spend the whole day doing exactly what other people tell you so there's no freedom involved, then it's going to be a bit of a struggle to get out of bed, isn't it? If you've ever experienced Mondayitis you know exactly what I mean!

So, why do you? Have you ever wondered that? What gets you out of bed when you know the day is not going to be a particularly enjoyable day? The answer is your power values. They're your drivers and motivators. They're also the side of us we tend to hide from other people; the side we wouldn't want to stand up and admit to in public. The purpose of this process is to help you see that power values are simply part of who you are and not a bad thing or personality flaw. The beauty of fulfilling your power values is that you actually achieve your golden values as well. So, you actually get what you want by being true to yourself. How often do we forget that simple truth? Plus you can harness your power values, putting them to good use so that it is even easier to get that business success or whatever you desire to move forward in your life.

Are you ready to play?

The key to success in this is to adhere to the three simple rules:

1. No shame.
2. No guilt.
3. No self-judgement when you're working through these exercises.

So, examples of power values are things like superiority, control, attention, validation, being right, money, unique, and special. You might have different names for these, or different interpretations of these words. It doesn't really matter as long as you are very clear what that value means to you. Like I said, you're not going to stand up in public and say, "Yes, my most important value is attention". They'll probably say, "Yes, we can see that!"

Let's have a look at an example from one of my clients. We were looking at her values overall, and her power values were revealed as 1) control, 2) being right, and 3) validation. I'll go through and explain how to work out yours in a minute, but firstly I want you to see how they tie in with your golden values and how you can put them to optimum use. That way it'll be easier for you to stick to the rules of no shame, no guilt, and no self-judgement.

For my client, let's call her Fran, control was all about freedom. When she was in control of her business, in control of how the office ran, then she had the freedom that came from the financial wealth. She also had the head space to know immediately when something was amiss so she could take action to correct the situation. Because Fran was organised, she didn't have to worry about remembering that and not forgetting this, she could think of something else – so she had mental freedom as well as physical freedom. She had systems in place, which meant that if she wanted to go off and have a lunch meeting with someone and it went half an hour longer, there was no problem. The business continued in her absence. If her son was sick, she had no problem in taking time off work because her staff are well-trained and followed the systems in place.

So, to some, perhaps Fran was a 'control freak'. That seems to be a common term applied by the disorganised to the organised. But seriously, she just had the systems in place to give herself more freedom. Having her power value of control fulfilled not only gave her freedom, it also gave her staff freedom. Because they knew what to do and when, that freed them up. They just got on with their job, they knew what the boundaries were, and they knew their responsibilities and the consequences of not performing. That gave them the freedom to set their own workload and work at their own pace. Knowing they were trusted and appreciated by Fran assisted in their smooth autonomy.

Fran's family and friends also gained freedom from her being a good organiser. They could rely on her to get things sorted, delegate so they could contribute in a meaningful way, or allow them to just relax and enjoy the ride.

Her second power value was being right – she loved being right! Therefore, she checked her facts and highly valued lifelong learning. She invested heavily in reading, researching, and in both professional and personal development. The obvious benefit to her clients and staff was that they could ask her a question and know that she absolutely had the right answer. And if she didn't, she wouldn't lie, she wouldn't bluff. She'd find out the answer or at least point them in the right direction so they could find the answer themselves.

Naturally, that flows over in advice for family and friends. And of course, it's not about claiming to be right, no matter what the cost. There's that balance too. You love being right so you find out the answers and check your facts, but if you prove that well, actually that wasn't the correct information, you weren't right that time, you acknowledge and move on. A wise soul also knows that both sides of a disagreement can be right, in their own realities, which they are. The solution is simply to accept and respect that each other has a different opinion.

Fran's third highest power value was validation. So for her, it was really important to feel that people knew who she was and appreciated that.

So, the opposite of that – the flipside of validation – was love, because when she was feeling validated she felt great about herself. Because she felt great about herself, she didn't need to waste time and energy looking inside for faults. Her focus could shine brightly out, and she had more to give people. Does that make sense? Basically, she was filling her own well until it overflowed. So as long as people in the workplace and her family and friends did things to show that they really appreciated and understood who she was and admired her, she just overflowed with love to share all around.

For Fran, the power value of control was matched with freedom, being right was balanced with knowledge and life-long learning, while fulfilled validation filled her life with love.

Can you see how having your power values, the dark side of your personality, honoured, you get the golden side fulfilled, and all those in your life benefit as well?

TIME TO CHANGE EXERCISE: SO WHAT ARE YOUR POWER VALUES?

There are different ways to reveal yours, but I found the most effective way is to ask you a couple of questions, and from there we can tease out what yours might be. So, you might like to have paper and pen on hand to make notes for yourself, and write here in the book. The first question is: what do you spend your money on? After the basics, what do you do with what's left over, your disposable income? It could be clothes, seminars and books, travel, or it could be savings or mortgage offset. Let's have a look at those four first.

Say you spend most your spare money on clothes, including shoes and other accessories. Why? What's important to you about those clothes? You might say, "I like to look nice". So, why is it important to you to look nice? Is it that you're getting – remember, no shame, no judgement, and no guilt about these – the attention you like? Do you like people telling you how good you look? Is it that you feel a little bit superior because you're the most beautifully or expensively dressed person in the room? Or maybe you're into really quirky, unusual fashion statements or unusual jewellery? If that's you, maybe you want to feel like you're unique. You want to feel like you're one-of-a-kind and stand out in that way. It could be any of those three. It could be a combination.

Write down what resonates for you and know if you have a really strong resistance – that couldn't possibly be me, no, no, no ... no way! Well then absolutely, chances are it is. Denial is a great sign.

So, what else do you spend your money on? Maybe you're into seminars and books and CDs and are always learning things. Why do you want to learn more? Is it because you love being right, like my client? Is it because when you know more than others you feel superior? Is it the attention you get by knowing answers or mixing with the seminar scene? Particularly if you go to the seminars where everyone's getting hugs all the time. Or maybe that's the case of validation? People actually see who you are and say that you're okay. Have a little think about what it is for you, remembering no shame, no guilt, and no self-judgement.

What else do you spend your money on? Travel? So for travel, it could be that you love the cultural experiences such as the food, meeting the local people or other travellers. It might be the sense of freedom. Whatever it is for you, what's actually underneath that? What does it actually get you? Is it because you're getting attention because you're going off to all these exciting places and you come back and share your photos? Do you feel a bit unique because you are the only person in your circle that actually travels to Ethiopia or Kathmandu?

Do you perhaps feel a little bit superior because you can travel overseas, and you've seen so much more of the world than those other people? Do you feel superior because you've really roughed it and survived? Or that the only stars you'll sleep under are the five on a hotel sign? Check in with yourself about who you talk to, what you talk about, and how you promote your travels to others. What do you highlight and why? The luxurious accommodation or the squat toilets?

Remember: no shame, no guilt, and no self-judgement. We're just working out what your power values are so you can understand yourself more, and harness their power. What's beneath the gloss and what really drives you? Check back over the list of power values I gave you earlier.

The second powerful question you can ask to find out what your power values are is: what frustrates you really quickly and why? For example, you might say, "Idiot drivers. I hate the way they just cut you off as if you're not there. It's dangerous". Yes it is. What aren't you getting when they cut you off? Is it that you're not being validated as a person, let alone a good driver? You're not being visible and they don't even see you. Is it because you're not in control? You can drive as safely as you can but you can't control that other idiot who might smash into you. So, perhaps you have a sense of lack of control? Is it to do with being right? You're driving this way but they are choosing to drive a different way, so does that make you wrong? You know the road rules, but by ignoring them he is implying you no longer have the moral high ground. It could be any of those, or a combination.

What frustrates you? You might say, "People interrupting". What aren't you getting when people interrupt you and finish your sentences? Control is one. You're not even allowed to finish what you're going to say. It could be being right because if they're finishing your sentences they obviously know more than you. Maybe it's validation; you are not being heard. They don't hear who you are and what you're about.

What is it for you? Maybe you hate the kids and your partner making a mess in the house; leaving their dirty clothes everywhere, not putting the toilet seat down, dishes in the sink, whatever it is. So, what aren't you getting when they're making a mess in the house? Control springs to mind, but often it's actually more than that. It could be that you're not feeling superior because the house is messy and therefore if someone came in they wouldn't think that you were an amazing housekeeper. Maybe it's the attention. Maybe it's the validation. If they're treating you like the housemaid rather than picking up after themselves, it could be something along those lines.

So what is it for you? Normally, with my coaching clients, we complete a process which we fine tune to work out the top three, but if you've got between three and five written down, the chances are that's pretty close to your top ones anyway.

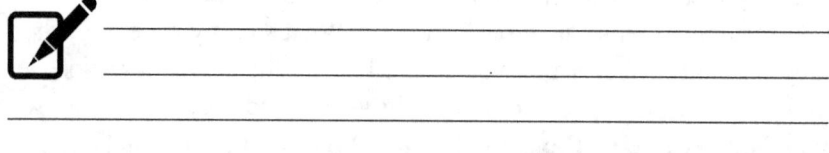

How do you put this knowledge to good use? Firstly, just as in the client example I gave you earlier, it's important to identify your flip sides to your power values. For example, if your power value is validation then its opposite could be love. If it's being right, is lifelong learning or education the match? Control might give you security. Being right might give you a feeling of security. Attention might mean love for you, or a sense of self or belonging.

So, consider the opposite side of each of your power values, and just know that by having your power values fulfilled, you automatically get the other side fulfilled and benefit all the people around you.

Power Values	Golden Values	Benefits To Others
_____	_____	_____
_____	_____	_____
_____	_____	_____

As discussed earlier, your power values are your true drivers, your true motivators, so it would be a shame not to put all awareness to good use. There are four ways I'll discuss here, and you may find more for yourself.

1. Harness your power values to your dream goals.
2. Harness to your daily tasks.
3. Use your awareness to increase your personal power.
4. Use your awareness to improve communication with others.

1. HARNESS YOUR GOALS

If motivation has been a problem, you'll love this. Hopefully, you've some goals written down. If you haven't it's not too late. Grab a pen and write three down, right now. Make them specific, timely and realistic, for example, 'Release 20kgs by 30 June 2014' rather than the vague 'Lose weight'. Going to the toilet will achieve the latter, temporarily! Likewise, finding a 10 cent coin means 'Have more money' is achieved, when probably you meant, 'Earn $100,000 or more in 2014'.

MY TOP 3 GOALS

1. _____

_____

_____

2. _____

_____

_____

3. _____

_____

_____

The power of written goals, as opposed to ones kept only in your head, is well documented and cannot be underestimated. For example, your goal might be to grow your business by 30 per cent, or finish that degree you've been studying part-time forever, or find a loving partner to marry, or release 20 kilos, or increase your income by 50 per cent per annum. Whatever it is for you, if you find enough examples of how achieving that goal fulfils your power values, then absolutely you will find that motivation comes really easily.

So what do you actually need to do? As you know, different results come from changing at least one factor, and that takes action. Absolutely allocate time for dreaming in your life, imagining the impossible becoming possible, and then turn those dreams into reality by setting goals and taking action. If you are ready to get different results, choose a number. The larger the number the more committed you are to achieving the outcome, but be realistic – you won't really write one million ways, so perhaps start with 100 ways, or 250 ways.

For example: One hundred ways of increasing my income by 50 per cent fulfils my values of attention, superiority, being right and validation.

1. My rapid income growth gets me attention.
2. I'll feel superior for making more money when others are struggling.
3. It'll prove my way is right.
4. I can attend more seminars and learn even more to be the expert.
5. More exciting overseas holidays.
6. Beautiful new clothes to wear to functions so I get compliments.
7. I'll have more money to buy better gifts.
8. I'll feel great being acknowledged for donating more for my charity.

And so on, brainstorming, writing down whatever comes to mind, knowing there aren't any wrong answers. Keep going until you have your 100, then write five more, just to prove you've more inside than you thought. Re-read your list, and for each one picture yourself there, doing that thing, hearing the compliments, feeling totally validated or superior or special, noticing how great it feels to have people acknowledge you are right. Observe exactly how your life has changed. By doing that for each one of those ways on your list, you're really cementing in the value of that goal.

What's that you say? Don't have time? Oh well, you're obviously not uncomfortable enough in your current situation to make change a higher priority. What would put you in enough pain to make the time? Losing your job? A heart attack? Your spouse leaving you? You have the same number of hours in the day as everyone else, and how you spend those hours is a direct reflection on your values, both power and golden. It's up to you whether you take preventative or proactive action now, or wait until you have no choice.

Motivation comes easily then as it's like your crew, aka your unconscious mind, is saying, "Oh okay, I get it! So that's why you want more money. That's why you want to ditch those extra 20 kilos. I see, that's why you want that relationship – because you'll feel special, validated and have much more control. Let's go for it". Then you start taking action and getting into the flow of your goal.

2. HARNESS TO YOUR DAILY TASKS

You won't wake up one day and suddenly find your dream goal has been achieved without you having taken any action at all. Your daily To Do list is actually where the magic starts happening. That's because the present is the only space that is real, and it's in the present that you create your future by thinking those thoughts, choosing how to act, the meaning you give to events and the feelings you hold on to or let go of.

Ideally, the only items on your To Do list are those which directly relate to achieving your big dream goals, one step at a time. Sometimes that one step needs to be a giant leap, if there's no landing space between. If having a happy loving family in your own lovely home is one of your goals, then of course family and home maintenance issues are necessary steps in that situation. If you were to colour code your items to do, how many would be for you and your goals, and how many for others? Try it now if you like. I'll wait here until you get back ...

Interesting results? I discuss boundary setting more in Chapter 7, Putting the 'I' Back Into your LIFE.

You've got a list of all of those things that you 'should' do. Maybe it's a list for around the house, maybe it's a list at work. Maybe your list is buried under that pile of papers to read, sort, file or dump that you haven't got around to. The pile that sits on the desk or in the corner glowering at you. So just tie those little irritating tasks to your power values and watch them disappear.

If you don't have a list, unless it's because you are totally up to speed in absolutely every area of your life, make a commitment to write one, ideally divided at least into 'home' and 'business'. The beauty of a list is that it takes all of that white noise out of your head. By white noise I mean all of the chatter about 'must not forget', 'must remember', 'have to', 'should', 'what if I forget?' etcetera. All you then have to remember is to look at your list each day, and choose the three most important tasks to do. The important ones are the ones which will create the most difference in your life should you do them, and often they are the ones that are outside your comfort zone. Brian Tracey refers to them as "frogs", recommending you "eat your frog" first thing in the morning, then the rest of your day will improve dramatically because you've done the worst thing first.

Ask yourself: how will clearing my desk help me fulfil my value of being even more in control? And answer yourself with all of the reasons, as many as you need to feel motivated to start cleaning it up. Allow yourself to clean up right there and then. Rather than looking at your messy desk and at some level feeling, "Oh no, there's too much to do, I can't cope, I haven't got enough time", you'll feel virtuous about your clean desk, feel like everything is under control, be able to find paperwork quickly and easily, work more efficiently, therefore make more money.

So, go through your To Do list, cross off everything that only serves someone else. Be aware of the consequences and make other interim arrangements if necessary. Next, for every other task you've been putting off find a way to tie it to your power values. Fulfilling your power values becomes your driver, your motivator, to actually get in there and get it done. It works because at the unconscious level you'll understand the benefits of completing the task. Those benefits will often outweigh the fears and self-doubts that occur when stepping out of your comfort zone, for example, making follow up calls to potential clients.

After doing this exercise with one of my clients, he reported back the result was amazing. He'd finally cleaned out his fish tank. All the weeks and weeks of nagging by his wife hadn't made any difference. The fish were gasping for oxygen but it hadn't made a difference. All we did was reframe the issue and link the task to his power value of being right and suddenly it was easy. His resistance disappeared. His fish were so grateful.

Cleaning a fish tank may seem insignificant, but divorces are created out of a series of insignificant, irritating issues which build up and become a battle ground of moral superiority on the base of unfulfilled love strategies. Why do you think his wife chose to persist with the frustration of reminding him, the nagging, to see the fish potentially die, and have an ugly, slimy fish tank in their dining room, rather than clean the tank out herself? If she had, how would their relationship dynamics have changed? What would you have done in that situation? Why?

3. USE YOUR AWARENESS TO INCREASE YOUR PERSONAL POWER

The third way you put your awareness of your power values to good use involves three steps to increasing your personal power. It's a combination of using your values and being aware of yourself and how you respond to other people.

Step one is to be aware.

Step two is to be aware. (This is not a printing error.)

Step three is to smile and switch.

Let's have a look at what these mean in more detail.

The first step: be aware. For example, you catch yourself getting frustrated with someone. So, the first step is to be *aware* of the fact you are frustrated, and specifically what you are frustrated about. Which of your power values is being violated? Is it that you're not getting control when they do that? Is it that you're not feeling special, or you're not feeling validated? You're certainly not feeling superior. What is it for you in this particular circumstance?

Once you're aware of the violated power value then you go onto the second step which is also to be aware. In this step, you step outside of yourself and have an objective look at the situation. For example, you might think, "Oh, okay. So when I'm frustrated because I'm not feeling in control or frustrated because I'm not feeling validated, that's what I do. Put my hands on my hips. Look at my face. Ooh, listen to my language! I wonder if I'm going to stamp my foot?!"

Have you ever laughed at the faces toddlers pull when they are about to have a dummy spit? And have you ever glimpsed your own face in a reflection when you are being angry and frustrated? They are very similar and equally funny in the big scheme of things. That's where the third step comes in. So you simply need to acknowledge, observe then smile or laugh at yourself in your awareness, and then step into your personal power by choosing an alternative way to act.

So, they are the three steps to healing yourself, and it all happens in a second or two. Be aware – in other words, be aware that you are feeling frustration, anger or hurt. Notice which of your power values are being violated. The second 'be aware' is to step outside of yourself, notice what you're doing, what you say, the thoughts, how your body is. The third step is to choose to smile and switch behaviours. Or, if you want to continue, at least do it with awareness and enjoy the ride. Sometimes being a big, scary, angry monster can be great fun.

"Your life is now, not tomorrow, so live your life now. Let go and grow."

Sue Lester

4. USE YOUR AWARENESS TO IMPROVE COMMUNICATION WITH OTHERS

Now, a word of warning, once you've worked out what your power values are, please, please, please don't share them with partners or friends, unless they have completed the process too. I know this from experience – myself and clients – no matter how much someone loves you, at some point they'll throw it back in your face. For example,

"That's just you doing your control thing again. You just want to be right". They may already say something similar, but doing it with insider knowledge is particularly hurtful, so just keep it to yourself. Relish your own self-awareness and acknowledge how you're putting it to good use managing your own behaviour. You'll notice that when you're having a conversation with someone that's not going right, if you can be aware of what's happening inside your own head and change it then you can change the whole dynamics. You make your communication more effective, and ideally it becomes a win-win for both of you.

Obviously everyone, no matter what age, has power values as unconscious drivers. The fourth way of utilising their power is to be aware of other people's potential power values. For example, if someone reacts to your words or actions unexpectedly, pause a moment to consider which of their potential power values you just stomped on. You may or may not be able to immediately make amends, but your awareness stops the situation from worsening because you've taken it personally. And yes, like any knowledge, this can be used for good or evil. The assumption in writing this book is that all I share will be used ethically to improve the greater world as a whole.

This understanding power values is part of increasing your personal power by understanding and accepting your light and dark sides. There are at least two sides of you, and understanding what really drives you absolutely gives you more control over your life and the results you get personally and in business. Your self-awareness and acceptance can make your life a happier one because as we said, life is only real in the present moment. Your life is lived moment by moment, so the more moments you can make happy and satisfying, the happier and fulfilling your life will be as a whole.

Understanding comes with the responsibility of taking control back for how you live your life. But what if you don't know who you are anymore, let alone where you want to go? The next chapter is particularly relevant for you if you feel at times you've lost the 'I' out of your life.

KEY POINTS

» Your values are simply what is most important to you.

» How you spend your time and money indicates your top values.

» Your power values, your 'dark side', are your true drivers.

» Harnessing your power values to your goals gets results faster.

"Don't be afraid to take a big step if one is indicated; you can't cross a chasm in two small jumps."

David Lloyd George

SEVEN.
PUTTING THE 'I' BACK INTO YOUR LIFE

In the last chapter you identified your power values and now know your true drivers and motivators, but there's no point revving up your engine if you don't know where you are headed. Do you really know who you are and what you want? Perhaps you have become so busy being someone else's wife, mother, daughter, sister, friend, colleague or boss that you've lost touch with who you are? Do you remember being happier, braver and more adventurous, perhaps travelling the world, and now hardly recognise yourself in the mirror? Is it time to put the 'I' back into your life? Yes, I think so too! Let's explore how to do that by firstly identifying who you are, secondly clarifying what you need more and less of in your life, and thirdly learning how to retrain yourself and your loved, and not-so-loved, ones.

 **TIME TO CHANGE EXERCISE**

One of the first exercises I do with new clients is a questionnaire specifically designed to identify the deeper underlying root of the presenting problems, to pin-point significant events and tap into the client's own unconscious wisdom, bringing to the surface their own solutions and courses of action. The first question, on the surface, is an innocent one designed to break the ice and identify themes to use in subsequent metaphors and processes. It is also the one question most likely to produce either silence or tears.

It is, "What are you passionate about or enjoy doing most?"

What's your answer?

_____

_____

A common answer is, "I don't know anymore". My response is, "What did you used to enjoy? What do you do when you are not working now?". How often do you do those things in *your* answer?

_____

_____

Is that enough?

_____

_____

What would you prefer?

_____

_____

What are you saying is stopping you from having your preference?

_____

_____

Much of my work with clients is removing the head trash blocking or fouling their life paths. They are freed to step up and take action by changing the stories they tell themselves about it being too hard, or there's not enough time or money, or they're not smart enough or rich enough, not beautiful enough, not sexy enough. Really, all of that comes down to, underneath at a deep, unconscious level, that feeling of, "I'm not worthy", or "I'm not enough". And sometimes, for some people, it's safer to actually stay in the rut because what if? What if – yes, it's uncomfortable there in the mud, but what if I step up and find that I'm really not enough? And that's one of those what ifs where we get stuck because what if we try and we don't end up with the results we want? So therefore, we don't take action. One of the most disempowering duos is those two little words, what if.

Until you can change those deep, unconscious beliefs, a simple but effective interim measure is this exercise. You're doing the what ifs and you're picturing something negative. It really doesn't feel good and your anxiety is rising. Knowing the vision is purely in your imagination, it's not real, ask yourself, "What if it doesn't happen like that? What if it happens exactly the opposite way and I do get something wonderful out of it? How would that feel?"

Focus on that desirable alternative, particularly the feelings as they negate the anxiety, and gently correct yourself if your mind strays. Know it's absolutely true that if you can imagine the negative what ifs, that horrible failure, doom and gloom, then absolutely, you've got a great imagination. That's a powerful talent, but use it for good, not evil. Imagine what you would really like to see and take action, no matter how small, to make that start happening in your life, simply because you can.

I have a frog story to share with you. I can't remember where I originally heard the basis of this story years ago, so here is my version:

It was one of those beautiful blue sky days in the country with the birds singing and the cows chewing away. There was a country road. You know those country roads with the two ruts where the tyres have worn into the ground and there's grass in the middle. It had been raining often and there were occasional puddles in the ruts. A frog was jumping along in the grass beside the country road. He noticed a particularly muddy puddle and, peering over the rut edge, spotted another little frog. He thought he recognised him from tadpole school, so called out, "Hey, how are you doing?". The little frog in the puddle just grunted at him.

"What are you doing down there?"

"Oh, I'm just hanging around. Getting by."

"Well, why don't you come up here? There are great flies up here. Be nice to have your company."

"No. I'm okay. It's not so bad."

And the friendly frog thought, "Okay, I'll try again ..."

"Come on up. I know this great pond. There are lily pads, lots of flies, and clean deep water. I'll show you the way."

The response was, "I'm not ready yet. It's all right for you. Besides, it was good enough for my family so it's good enough for me."

The little friendly frog just shrugged his little frog shoulders and hopped away to the lily pad pond. And so, you can imagine the little friendly frog's surprise a few days later at the pond when he turned around to see the little grumpy frog from the puddle.

"Hello, great to see you! Hmm, if you don't mind me asking, what happened to change your mind about getting out of the rut?"

And the grumpy frog looked a bit sheepish – which is a fine effort for a frog – and said, "A truck came along".

Who do you know who's waiting for a truck to come along before moving out of his or her rut?

A NOTE ON PROCRASTINATION

Sometimes, perhaps quite often, you know what you 'should' be doing, yet you don't. Why? I find it is usually one of three reasons: values, fear or timing.

The values issue is that it simply isn't important enough for you to stop doing whatever you are currently doing instead. Perhaps it's on your list because it is important to someone else. Perhaps you are using inaction in a power play to rebel or punish? You have a choice to make it important by tying it to your power values, delegating / outsourcing or crossing it off your list. It's wasting energy if you are feeling guilty or it's taking up brain space thinking about not doing it. If you are using passive-aggression, stop, and find a more empowering way to communicate your true feelings.

Fear is a powerful procrastinator as it keeps you safe from failing or achieving or getting attention or proving yourself wrong – you are actually more capable than you tell yourself. Identify your underlying fear by asking yourself what is the absolute worst outcome from completing this? What you are aware of that you can change. Sometimes the awareness itself is enough of a reality check to put it into perspective.

Timing can be used as an excuse to disguise a fear-based reason, but is different. Perhaps the timing isn't yet right as you haven't finished your due diligence, processed the information in your creative juices, had that extra insight to turn it into extraordinary, or looked after your body enough so you have the energy needed to succeed well.

Think about what you've been procrastinating about; consider which of these applies, and what action you will now take.

We'll discuss trucks and ruts further in Chapter 9, Pain and Dis-ease, and Chapter 10, Weighing Heavily On Your Mind, and Chapter 12, Relationships Refreshed.

For now, let's get on with helping you get back in touch with who you are.

TIME TO CHANGE EXERCISE: IDENTIFYING 'ME'

Who are you? How do you identify yourself? Write some answers here to finish off the sentence: "I am _____".

_____

_____

_____

_____

Have a look at your answers. What do you notice? Are they all, or mostly, roles? It is very common for women in particular to identify themselves by the roles they play in their lives, for example wife, mother, daughter, sister, friend, businesswoman etcetera.

To illustrate this you would write your roles on spokes coming out from the central hub, which is 'Me'.

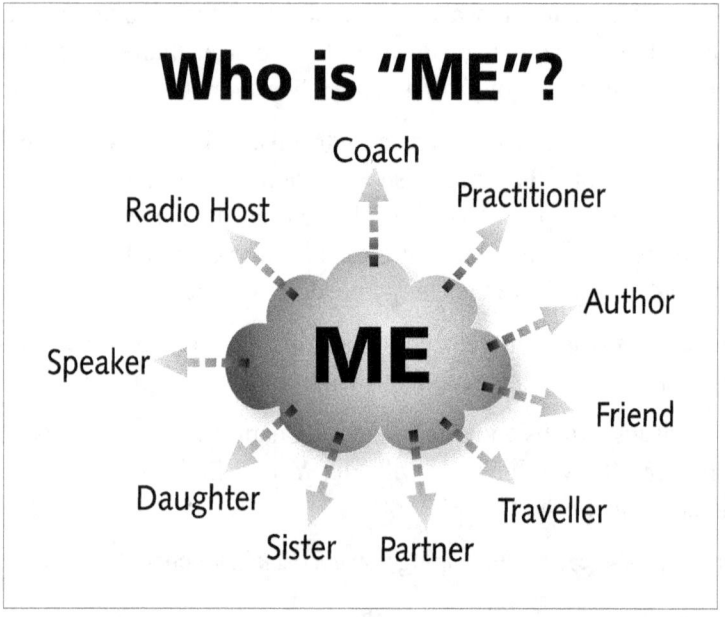

The danger of identifying yourself only by roles is that roles disappear or become less significant in your life. For example, your children grow up into the independent, capable adults you hoped for, in their own loving relationships, and need you less in the mothering role. Who are you when you are not being a wife, daughter, employer etcetera? If there is nothing much in the hub, your circle of life collapses into an identity crisis. That's part of the reason why it was so common for men to work extremely hard their whole lives, then be lost emotionally, mentally and physically on retirement without that work identity. A shortened life span followed all too often.

So who is the Me inside the hub? Your personality, interests, talents, dreams, strengths and weaknesses all belong there. Aim to write at least 50 words that identify the real you, and ideally write many more. Who are you? Have fun playing with this! Use lots of colours and pictures on a piece of chart paper if you wish. Who is the secret you? How would others describe you? You are a multi-faceted being, so write them all down. Think of each role and what you have that makes you good in that role.

You may notice some words will contradict each other, and that is perfectly fine. Write both down. You are simply human, dark and light, so naturally will be stronger in some areas of your life than others. Know too that for every negative you write there is a hidden positive. Look for that positive and bring it to light by writing it down.

Likewise, for every positive there can be an underlying negative. For example, in my teens and 20's I prided myself on my honesty. However, I was honest to the point of being hurtful or tactless at times, and conveniently forgot that I told white lies like everyone else. Being a dreamer can be both a source of creativity and a source of stagnation, of slow progress. A helpful or generous person can also be a doormat or gullible. Use this awareness of both sides as a safety or reality check so Me is a fleshed-out real person.

Who is the "ME" supporting your roles?

Value Freedom, Growth & Honesty
Adventurer   Loyal   Quick Wit   Optimistic
Speed Read   Recharge alone   Passionate
Love Nature   Courageous
Spiritual yet Earthy   **ME**   Catalyst of Change
Undervalue my Achievements   Enjoy Speaking Gigs
Writer   Impulsive   Creative   Intuitive
Vivid off-beat Imagination

How do you feel having identified Me? Ideally, you are feeling much more present and whole, and have at least a spark of excitement about recapturing your life.

As you look over Me, identify some parts you'd like to strengthen, and in doing so bring the fun and life back into your life.

Can they be done with your spouse and / or children, with friends new and old, or better done by you? Remember, just because you want change doesn't mean others in your life do, and there may or may not be resistance There's more about boundary setting and maintenance later in this chapter.

The key for now is to remember that others ultimately benefit from you being the very best, happiest, fulfilled you possible. Your children will choose relationships and parenting styles based on what you have role modelled for them. Are you living the life you'd like your children to have? Know it's never too late to make positive changes, as long as you are breathing!

> *"In the end, it's not the years in your life that count. It's the life in your years."*
>
> *Abraham Lincoln*

TIME TO CHANGE EXERCISE: FIRST STEPS

What are your first three steps to be completed by when? For example, book a dance class by Friday, hire a babysitter once a month, switch off the laptop at 5:00pm Fridays, start a gratitude journal today, book a Success Map session for next week. Write them down here and in your diary.

1. _____
_____

2. _____
_____

3. _____
_____

What would you like to let go of? For example, being lonely, telling myself I'm shy.

_____
_____
_____

What will you replace them with? For example, asking an old friend out to lunch, joining a Meet Up interest group, be my own best friend with self-talk, mindset coaching etcetera.

_____
_____
_____

KEY POINTS

- » Balanced people have both positive and negative traits.
- » A positive trait can be negative in some circumstances, and vice versa.
- » Remember that others ultimately benefit from you being the very best, happiest, fulfilled you possible.
- » Until you know and love who you are, you will never be content.
- » Live your life, not someone else's version of what it should be, or what you think someone else thinks it should be.
- » Procrastination is due to a values clash, fear or timing.

PUTTING THE 'I' BACK INTO YOUR LIFE

"Even if you're on the right track, you'll get run over if you just sit there."

Will Rogers

But remember...

"Standing your ground is progress when you're battling a hurricane."

David Weinbaum

EIGHT.
DE-STRESS FOR SUCCESS

What I'm really passionate about, the thing that gets me bouncing out of bed every day, is seeing everyday people break through their boundaries and transform their lives. They gain healthier lifestyles, thriving businesses, better relationships, and often the financial peace of mind that follows. Most importantly, they start liking and valuing themselves.

The thing is, you really can't have all those things if you are stressed to the eyeballs – alienating everyone around you with your irritability and bad moods. Your mood affects your ability to think clearly and really connect with your team and your clients, so your business suffers and you end up making yourself sick, literally, with worry. Chances are your relationship is also sick, though you might not notice until your spouse files for divorce, or you come home to an empty house. And I mean empty as in stripped of everything, as happened to a client. Understandably, he was devastated.

I had my own personal experience stressing myself sick in my early 20's. I played my squash fixtures grand finals and won, on my birthday. When I'd sobered up the next day I loaded up my car with the remains of my married life and left town to drive six hours to my parents' home. On arrival I was so stiff I had to be helped out of the car. My joints had painfully frozen, and it was terrifying to be in so much pain I couldn't walk properly.

I can still vividly see the doctor's grey eyes as he read out my test results and his forecast for my life. The tests showed I had rheumatoid arthritis. The doctor said this meant I'd be on painkillers the rest of my life and possibly end up in a wheelchair. If you've seen me speak on stage you'll know that obviously I'm not in a wheelchair. Since then I've trekked all over the world, including Nepal three times to an altitude of more than 5000m, and I walked across the Australian Simpson Desert with 16 camels. That was 27 days walking up and down over sand dunes. I'll share how I changed my destiny with you later in Chapter 9, Pain and Dis-ease.

Just the other day I heard from a client I worked with three years ago. At that stage she was suffering from panic attacks. They had seemingly started out of the blue a year before while she was on a train going home from work. She was only able to work limited hours from home, and could no longer drive a car or go shopping in malls and shopping centres by herself. Her marriage was suffering, and of course, so were her finances. She felt horribly guilty about her almost zero tolerance level with her children. She said she felt overwhelmed and just so stupid that she kept having the attacks.

During our sessions we identified that she had overloaded herself with her assumptions of other people's expectations of her being the successful career woman, super-mum and a sexy wife, to the point where she started having melt-downs. Underneath those expectations was a sense of having to prove that she was good enough, and the beliefs that saying "No" was selfish and a sign of a bad person. There were also fears that if she changed her career path to one more child-friendly and personally fulfilling, she would be considered a failure. She is an intelligent, creative person so her active imagination, all of those what ifs, had frozen her with the panic attacks. I knew she had made huge progress when she turned up to one of our sessions with shopping bags! She is now driving again, by herself, has her family back, and is thriving in a new role in her new workplace.

It's as if I'm a guide who provides a map and a torch if you feel off track. I guess the thing that is different about me is that I'm a stronger believer in finding the true underlying reason for stress and change rather than just treating the symptoms or changing the surface source. It becomes an exciting journey of self-discovery, week by week.

You might think the main causes of stress are not enough time, not enough money, poor relationships and change. I believe there are three core underlying challenges for the people I work with:

1. Self-worth
2. Self-trust
3. Being present

The majority of stress issues stem from the cumulative effect of one or more of these, and once that is identified, lasting changes become so much easier.

SELF-WORTH

Just think about it, if you feel you don't have enough time, is it a self-worth issue? Are you:

- Valuing everyone else's needs over yours – never saying "No", never filling your emotional and physical well?
- Struggling with poor boundary setting and maintenance – being a doormat?
- Taking on huge or numerous tasks to prove you are good enough?
- Not taking the time to care for your health – food, water, fresh air, sunshine, exercise, rest, sleep, laughter and love?
- Not truly believing you are deserving or worthy of success, wealth, happiness, so not taking action, just to protect yourself from disappointment? Procrastination is your daily companion.
- Constantly concerned about what others may think of you?

The result is naturally a sense that there's not enough time for you to do all you feel you need to do, and bucket loads of frustration, disappointment, hurt and guilt.

SELF-TRUST

If you feel you don't have enough money, look at these self-trust issues.

- Losing touch with your intuition and having so many voices/thoughts scrambling in your head it ends up being white noise.
- Second guessing yourself, and being unable to make clear decisions.
- Taking someone else's advice, even when it doesn't feel right to you, and realising too late that you should have trusted yourself. (Poor investment choices show up here.)
- Not knowing who to trust anymore so either trusting everyone and getting disappointed and hurt, or trusting no-one, keeping them at bay emotionally, depriving yourself of love and friendship.
- Fear of change – of making the 'right' decision, being able to do things differently, being accepted in a new group.
- Inaction due to indecision, with opportunities for growth lost.

The result is confusion, indecision, overwhelm, hurt, loss of self-esteem and confidence, and an income level that mismatches your hopes.

That was certainly Alex's situation when he came to me for help with anxiety. His business was actually doing well, but Alex was bored and worried he would be spending the rest of his life running that business. What really lit his eyes up was share trading. He had developed a system which had been working extremely well for him over four years. However, it was paper trading, in that he had never actually bought or sold those shares. He said his head was filled with self-criticism and fears at the thought of doing that, even though he was tearing himself apart in his current business.

We identified the internal self-critical voice was actually repeating his father's beliefs about the lack of moral virtues and low intelligence of those who gamble irresponsibly, including all share trading. His father had strong beliefs that the only honest money came from hard work, and that life was meant to be a struggle, to make people stronger.

Once we (Alex and I working together) had cleared the excess fear out of his system, we could clarify what Alex's own beliefs and values were. This freed him to think clearly and make considered decisions about many aspects of his life. He understood the wisdom of never speculating more than you can comfortably lose, which is generally 10 per cent, and the value of multiple income streams. So he hired a top notch manager to ensure his existing business continued to thrive, then launched himself mindfully into his new share trading career using his system as honed over those previous four years.

I was delighted the day he shyly rolled up his sleeve to show me his stunning new diamond Rolex watch. To me, it meant he not only was successfully following his passion, more importantly he was now valuing himself enough to reward himself to a level that reflected his success.

Mindset shifts are not about installing unrealistic or unsafe beliefs. In Alex's case it was not about making him feel bullet-proof trading, it was to clear the white-noise of excess negative emotions and disempowering beliefs so he was able to think clearly, do his due-diligence, and function effectively in the changes he chose to make in his life.

Likewise, when another client begged me to help her lose weight I refused. I'm all for healthy weight and have helped countless women to shift their relationship with food to make habit changes easier, but this client was different because she was already under her ideal weight range. As an alternative I offered to help her shift her body image so it was more realistic and sustainable, and we also worked together on her self-esteem, self-identity and values, managing family expectations and boundary setting.

Her new self-belief enabled her to acknowledge and utilise her natural intelligence studying at university towards a new corporate career, which happened to match her family's values. As we progressed and her inner strength and self-belief increased, she identified who she really was and changed her studies to natural therapy. An easier and less prestigious option in her family's belief, but one that fulfilled her needs and sense of purpose.

It takes personal power and the associated strong sense of self to be able to stand firm against the criticisms, fears and doubts of loved, and not-so-loved, ones. Some of their motivation will come from wanting to protect you, for in their maps of reality your course of action is not safe or even comprehensible, or you are not seen as fitting that new role in their worlds.

It may be about jealousy, or a fear you will leave them behind or expect them to step up out of their comfy rut to follow you. So it's important to understand and accept that what is right for one is not right for all. It doesn't make you wrong, it just makes you fulfilled, and a step closer to being the very best you possible.

IS IT YOUR INTUITION OR SELF-DOUBT?

Your intuition is a powerful force, but if you've been practicing self-doubt, second-guessing yourself, and listening to your 'bitch', you're probably confused as to whether that message is your intuition or self-sabotage. By the way, the part of you which self-sabotages does have an underlying positive intention for you – protection. What are you protecting yourself from? It is valid in your current reality or based on an opinion of someone from the past?

This flow chart of my Expand Or Contract Test helps you decide if the message is intuitive or not, by tuning into your body. 'Expand' refers to the feeling you get when you make a good decision, are happy or loving. It's a relaxing, letting go type of feeling. 'Contract' is what your body does when you are afraid, frustrated or unhappy. It tenses, whether you are aware of it or not.

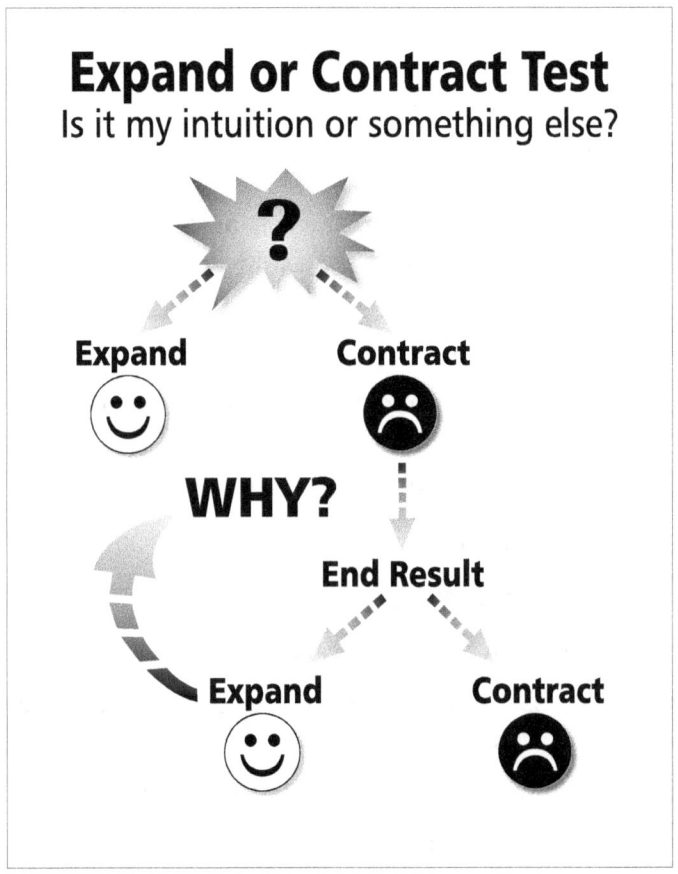

Let's run through an example together. Imagine you've the opportunity to attend a workshop. It sounds interesting and useful, but you're not sure.

- Think of attending the workshop. Do you expand or contract in your body?
- If you expand, then go for it, sign up.
- If you contract, then you need to work out if it's your intuition or fears getting in the way.

Go to the end result, for example, imagine yourself having finished the workshop. Do you expand or contract?

If you still contract, then it's not the right option for you at this point, even if others think so.

If you expand at the thought of having completed the workshop, then yes, it is the right thing for you to do, even if others disagree. You just need to work out why you were contracting initially so you can increase your self-awareness and deal with the underlying issue.

Here are the most common reasons why you might contract, and examples for this scenario.

Skill: You are worried you might have to do something new in front of the group.

Knowledge: It's a new topic and you feel out of your depth.

Resources: It costs money to attend.

Time: It's half your weekend.

Priority: Your family's needs appear more important than yours.

Past Experience: You went to a really high pressure workshop several years ago.

Other People's Stuff: Your husband scoffed at the topic.

Once you identify and resolve the underlying issues you can confidently make your choice to attend, and reap the benefits. Like any tool or technique, the more you use it, the easier and faster you get results.

BEING PRESENT

If you are experiencing relationship stress, anxiety or depression, chances are you haven't been present enough. That is, you are:

- Living in the past, rehashing, sifting through the ashes and pus, getting into the negative downward spiral of depression.

- Focussing on the person's negative behaviour in the past, imagining that behaviour being repeated in the future, and feeling how you would feel it did. (I bet you've had a fight with someone out there in the future in your own head too!)
- Living in the future, tormenting yourself with the negative what ifs.
- Frozen with fear, unable to act as you are stuck in the past or in the future where nothing is safe.
- Experiencing a lack of control as you can't fight or run away from what only exists in your imagination – your thoughts.

In the present you are normally safe and can relax. Each second of the present you can control how you choose to think, feel and act. Personal power, that is being centred, confident, knowing and liking who you are, is fully in the present.

Tom was man on a mission, determined to create wealth for himself and his family. He was often away, chasing leads for new clients, and when at home was usually behind the closed door of his study, plotting and planning for the future. He ignored ill health and kept pushing himself. One day an out of town appointment rescheduled at the last moment, and unusually Tom decided to head home early. He decided it would be fun to surprise his wife and children, so instead of driving around the back of the house like all family and friends did, he parked out front and rang the front door bell. He smiled in anticipation as he heard his four-year-old son race through the house to the door. His son appeared, solemnly looked him up and down, and then yelled, "Mum! There's a man at the door!".

Tom said he felt he'd been kicked in the stomach. His own son hadn't recognised him out of context. Our work together focussed on finding that life balance so he could keep his current wife and family to share his future with. This involved a shift in his unconscious blueprint to an image of a successful family businessman, and a values realignment. Once Tom realised he was in danger of not only losing his family but having to split his assets in a divorce, he decided it was a wise business decision to adjust the pace of his growth.

By valuing family time more and reconnecting with his loved ones, his stress levels reduced and his health improved. Improved health and energy meant he could be more productive in fewer hours. Once Tom learnt how to be more present with his clients, rather than having one eye on the next prospect, his business improved significantly through referrals and client retention.

In Jane's case she and her husband had raised their children together, and then chose different job and business paths, involving weekend and night shifts. Personally and professionally, they grew at very different rates, and over the years their marriage had dissolved into a convenient living arrangement without them noticing. Initially my coaching brief was to work on Jane's business management, including staff training and boundary setting, and locking her unconscious blueprint as a businesswoman.

Freed from that stress load and constantly being out in the future planning her business, Jane had time to notice the lack of connection with her husband in the present. She suddenly realised they only had their children and grandchildren in common, and very different ideas of how their relationship could be fulfilling. She explored so many ways to reconnect with her husband, but in the end, faced with his resistance to even acknowledge there was room for improvement, to be true to herself and how she wanted her life to be, she had to move out to move on.

The key point is: the only person you can change is yourself. In doing so, there is a ripple-on effect, which may or may not be a catalyst for change in others. It's your life, your choice. It's their lives, their choices.

If you both choose to share your journey together, then know a loving relationship that stands the test of time has respectful, mutual compromise as an integral ingredient. You can both be right without one having to be wrong. You are both right in your own realities.

Stress stemming directly from change, whether self-initiated or not, encompasses all self-worth, self-trust and taking control in the present issues.

So what to do?

There are three levels to de-stressing effectively:

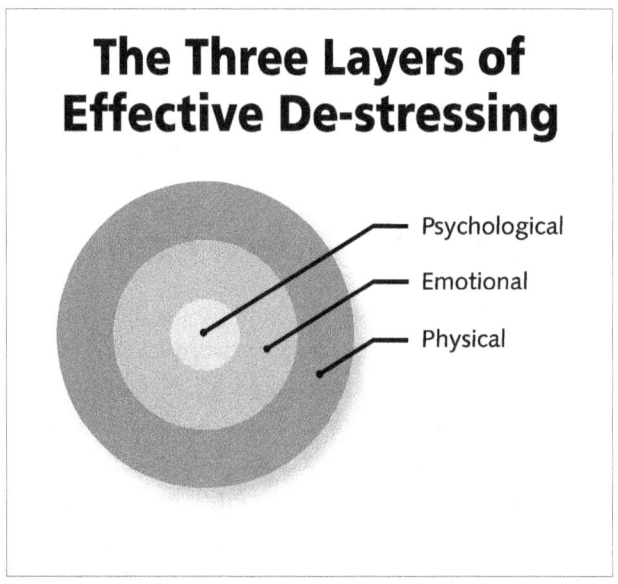

PHYSICAL DE-STRESSING

There are so many ways you can de-stress physically, and I'm sure you can list 20 off the top of your head without trying. Your list is likely to include exercise in its myriad of forms, from a walk around the block to Tai Chi to kite-boarding. Massages, particularly reflexology, can be extremely relaxing with the right therapist. If you are uncomfortable, don't like the way you are being massaged, or hate the music being played, for goodness sake, speak up. Unspoken resentment worsens your stress. Physical de-stressing also includes actively playing with your kids and pets, having fun, laughing, hugging, tickling and making love – only if you are a willing participant enjoying yourself.

In addition, getting yourself organised, from filing to getting your tax returns up to date and your home and work space de-cluttered, makes an enormous difference. Do those repair jobs around the house or hire someone to do them for you. Those little niggly things are being picked up on your unconscious radar and contribute to your overall feeling of being rushed, not having enough time, and not coping. Make your home and work spaces comfortable, efficient, and attractive to you.

And of course, remember to breathe 3:6 for instant calming. (Breathe in for a count of three and out for a count of six.) It's so effective because you start using your full lung capacity, rather than the shallow breathing of a stressed person, so increase the amount of oxygen flowing to your brain considerably.

EMOTIONAL DE-STRESSING

Often an outburst of strong, negative emotion is the first time you might acknowledge to yourself and others you are overly stressed. Yelling, snarling, bursting into tears, or a panic attack are signs of overflow. You've literally 'had it up to here' or 'had a neckful'. Of course, it's been accumulating over time, unprocessed and unreleased. The aim is for you to be able to feel and express a strong emotion in an appropriate way, learn from the experience, and let it go. To get to that point, often it's necessary to do a clearing process, with Neuro Linguistic Programming (NLP) for example, to clear the excess out of your system. I'm a firm believer in using processes that clear without you having to relive any trauma. You've gone through it once, and that was enough.

Next time you felt that emotion, anger for example, you feel the amount appropriate to the occasion rather than that amount on top of all that has been stored before. You then have a moment of choice in which you can decide how to respond rather than simply react. Of course, you can still be a big, scary, angry monster if you wish, but it'll be a conscious choice. Your children, partner and staff will love the difference!

One client's four-year-old said, "Mummy, I like you better now you're not angry anymore". It frees you to create happy memories with your children and loved ones. Emotional de-stressing also frees you from that endless chatter in your head, so you are able to think clearly and make more empowered decisions. Best of all, you are free to enjoy your minute, your hour, your day, your life in the present, which is life's gift to you.

The range of emotions we feel is vast, however, they are all variations on the big five: anger, sadness, fear, hurt and guilt. Imagine these emotions are like the layers of an onion, with anger on the outside, sadness beneath that, then fear, then hurt, and guilt in the centre. Each has a message for us, as do all emotions. The more positive ones like joy, contentment, love and happiness are telling us, "Great work, keep it up – more, more". They tell us we are connected, valued, loved, that we belong, are worthy and that we are enough. The big five are warnings that something isn't right, and that action is needed to stop the situation.

ANGER

Anger is a message that our boundaries have been crossed. Someone or something isn't playing by our rules, and we want them to stop. It can also be a protective mechanism when we are feeling fear, hurt or guilt – it becomes our very own anti-bandit screen, a bluff to hide our true feelings. Bullies are generally cowards inside. They know inside that they are inadequate, and it's only by putting others down they can feel superior, in the momentary surge of power. When you step into your personal power and stay calm in the face of someone's anger, it will often confuse him or her. In that calmer space you can negotiate your desired outcome, or at the least, express your perspective.

Anger can be externally or internally expressed, depending on what we were taught as children and how our role models expressed it. In some families it is safe to yell back at a parent. In others it definitely is not. Expressing anger externally can be seen as 'not nice', so it must be held inside, fermenting in a sulk. A client once told me she wasn't an angry person, never had been. She did, however, get the most savage tension headaches when her boundaries were crossed. Another told me he didn't feel anger either, just frustration – to the point he could punch through a wall! Know that frustration is simply a form of anger. Feeling and expressing anger is perfectly normal and okay, as long as you remain in control of yourself, in mind, body and language, while expressing it.

What were your childhood lessons about anger? How do you express it now, as an adult? Does that method serve you well?

SADNESS

Sadness is highlighting loss, both real and imagined. When someone or something leaves our life, we have the real loss of that person or thing physically gone. It's important to acknowledge and accept that sadness, but also to allow it to pass. It's not necessary for you to stop living as well. In fact you can honour his or her memory by living your life to the full and being as happy and fulfilled as possible, as someone who loved you would wish. Honour their memory with happy memories.

The imagined loss is all of the future memories we've created in our mind involving that person. This is where some become stuck. Playing and replaying the future memories that will never happen now with that person intensifies the sadness into pain. That's why a teenage girl can be so devastated when she splits up with her boyfriend of three weeks – she hasn't just lost someone to go out with that weekend, she's lost the years of romance, the beautiful house, the two point five children, and happily growing old together.

Actually, it's not just teenagers is it? We women are far more thorough in creating our future memories than men. I believe it stems back to those caveman days when the male could focus solely on the hunt, while the woman was constantly on the lookout for signs of food to gather, keeping an eye on the children, and trying to second-guess her mate's needs so he would continue to protect her and her children.

Her thinking, "He's silent! Does that mean he's angry? Did I say the wrong thing? What if I've hurt his feelings? If he's hurt he should tell me. What if he's really not happy and wants to leave, and is just waiting for the right moment? I bet that slut Rockette has been hanging around!".

Him thinking, "Wonder how Bob caught that rabbit?".

FEAR

Speaking of caveman days, fear was so much simpler and easier to deal with. Danger appeared; you felt fear, then either fought or ran away. If you weren't eaten, the danger disappeared, as did your fear. Your adrenal system settled back into neutral. Fear is a sign we need to prepare to take action, whether that is to go into battle or run for the hills. As we've evolved, so have our imaginations. Take a look around the room you're in. Isn't it simply astounding how much humans have created out of our imaginations? It's a long way from the cave, baby! In our imaginations we can travel far out into the future. We can also travel back in time, pick up a piece of the past and place it out in the future, then feel it as if it has happened again. We can time travel all in our heads. Amazing, isn't it?

You travel out into the future and imagine what might happen, based on your experiences in the past and what you've learnt from others. You use the power of your imagination to see, hear and feel yourself there, and one of two things happens. If it is a positive future event you are creating in your imagination, you'll feel great and will be more motivated to take action to make that image real. If it is a negative future event you are seeing, hearing and feeling, once again your body doesn't know the difference, so you will experience the tension as your body contracts with anger, hurt, fear or guilt. The future then becomes an unpleasant place to be, but you can't avoid the future if you are continuing to live, so the anxiety builds up.

So what to do? You need a two-pronged response that offers both an alternative future scenario and an expansive feeling to relax the contraction in your body.

MAGIC WORDS

The magic words to counteract the anxiety build-up are, "And what if it doesn't happen like that? How will that feel?".

The first sentence offers the idea that there is an alternative, more pleasant future scenario. The scary story isn't set in stone. The second sentence invites your body to experience the excitement, pleasure or happy, expansive feeling of that alternative reality.

Remember, none of it is real. Only this present moment is real. The rest you are simply making up in your head. You can choose to scare yourself or encourage yourself.

The reason I include clearing build-ups of excess negative emotion in my early work with new clients is to make this reality management so much easier. When you are in a calm, centred place you aren't buffeted by circumstances in the same way someone adrift is.

HURT

The emotion of hurt is felt when your expectations are not met. Those expectations may or may not be realistic in any other reality than yours. Someone didn't respond in the way you expected or hoped for, based on your needs and how you would have responded in the same circumstances. You didn't realise they had a different love language from you. They simply didn't understand what you wanted or needed. Perhaps your needs didn't match their values, so simply didn't even appear on their radar? Their perception of you and your abilities was different from what you would have liked.

Poor communication of needs, the assumption that if someone loves us they will instinctively know what to do and say, is the cause of much hurt in relationships. That instinctive knowing only occurs if their love language matches yours, or they have learnt over the years of trial and error. I discuss more about building successful relationships in Chapter 11, Relationships Refreshed.

MAGIC WORDS

There are five little words (not three) that can magically free you and heal hurt-based resentment. This solution acknowledges that each of us has our own reality, based on how we filter information through our senses. It also acknowledges we have our own preferred way of showing love.

If these are your questions: "How can he do that? I wouldn't! How can she say that? I wouldn't! How come he didn't do that? I would have for him!".

The only answer you need to give yourself is, "Because he (or she) is not me".

It's as simple as that. Once you stop expecting others to think and act as you, rather than themselves, you stop wasting energy on unrealistic expectations. You can find common ground and enjoy them for who they really are, rather than who you want them to be. Isn't that what we each really want, to be accepted and loved for ourselves?

GUILT

The lesson from guilt is that a moral or ethical boundary has been violated, either by you or another. For some, when the boundary has been violated by another, shame is a more relevant label for the emotion felt. Anger is a common response when people are feeling guilty. Emotional blackmail, whether consciously intentional or not, is designed to generate guilt then the desired action.

I've worked with clients who have carried guilt since the womb, and even before. Or have shouldered the burden of guilt for others or for actions long forgotten or forgiven by others.

The first time I was personally clearing excess guilt from my system using an NLP process (guided by another practitioner), the source of that guilt turned out to be the pain I caused my mother during my birth. I have since found out more about my birth story, and it was a long, painful labour. Six months ago, at what I thought was my mother's deathbed, I apologised for any pain I had caused even though I know it was never under my control. Her response was she would have gone through anything to have the daughter she always wanted, and that she will never regret having me. (Rest in peace Melda Meree Lester 12th October 1936 – 17th May 2013).

GUILT IS A HEAVY AND UNNECESSARY BURDEN

Part of releasing excess guilt and shame out of your system is forgiveness. When I first trained in NLP I was taught various processes to assist clients in forgiving others, including abusers of every kind. As I worked with more and more people, it became clear to me that forgiveness of others was a stumbling block to progress, and ultimately unnecessary.

From my experiences as a teacher, from working in a social enterprise with low socio-economic families, from my grassroots travels across the world, my own relationships, and from the darkest secrets clients have shared with me, I have developed a new belief. Abuse happens in all countries, in all socio-economic levels, in private and government sectors, at all age levels with perpetrators of all genders.

My firm belief is that the only person any one needs to forgive is oneself.

Underneath any feelings of guilt or shame there is that deep, niggling feeling that you should have, could have, done something differently. Once you can truly forgive yourself for not being perfect, you truly free yourself. You can let go and grow, free to enjoy life's adventures. Yes, stumbling at times as we all do, but able to pick yourself up to continue the fun.

I believe your purpose is to strive to be the very best you that you can be. One thing I am sure of is, like me, you will never be perfect while you are part of the human race – so relax and give yourself a break!

> *"Practice makes progress. Perfect isn't for us mere mortals."*
>
> Sue Lester

PSYCHOLOGICAL DE-STRESSING

You may now be committed to de-stressing your body regularly and have sought assistance to clear the excess, negative emotions out of your system. You are aware of your time travels, and are consciously using the magic words to keep your life, including relationships, in perspective. You are feeling so much better, yet there is still an underlying tension that grabs at you from the shadows. That's where the third, innermost level of effective de-stressing comes into play. This is the psychological level, where unconscious disempowering beliefs, including your unconscious blueprint™, reside.

No matter how much personal and professional development you do, significant changes won't last until you change at this level. If, at the deepest level, you believe you are not worthy (of love, success, wealth), or you are not enough (not smart, beautiful, slim, sexy or wealthy enough), then it will be true.

You live the life of the person you believe you are.

Working with clients I use a variety of NLP and other techniques to change the unconscious, disempowering beliefs of unworthiness or inadequacy. The result is a clearing of the way, self-sabotage turns into self-motivation, and the appropriate actions become easier to define and take.

TIME TO CHANGE EXERCISE: PSYCHOLOGICAL DE-STRESSING

Readers, you can start yourself by noticing self-talk. When are you most savage with yourself? Does it trace back to a belief of 'not worthy/deserving' or 'not enough'? If you (the captain) tell yourself you don't know, then take a moment to ask the question of your 'crew'. Ask then simply listen for the answer. It'll be there if you let it.

Next, go back over your life and find proof of the opposite. List all of your achievements, no matter how small you tell yourself they are. Ensure you include learning to walk and talk, read and write, – because some never do. If you run out of ideas, think of yourself 10 years ago and write down what you can do now that you couldn't then, for example, use a Smartphone.

Write down all of your good deeds, random acts of kindness, and regular thoughtfulness, particularly if you remember and acknowledge people's birthdays, for example. And all of the people you have ever shown love, kindness or friendship to. Now write down all of the people who have ever shown love or kindness or friendship to you, including the friendly lady at the corner shop who would give you an extra lolly for free. If you don't know a name, write 'friend in Grade Three' or 'lover #10,459', for example.

Now write down all of the people who have ever hurt you – physically, verbally, emotionally or financially. Now write down all of the people you have hurt in a similar way – physically, verbally, emotionally and financially. Ensure the number of examples are the same in each list. This is to balance your perspective, as you are neither better nor worse, simply living in your reality as each live in theirs. For example, a rapist can be bad in your reality, but not in his, and not in some other cultures or in times of war in some people's realities.

Next, write your own eulogy – seriously! What would you like to be said about you at your own funeral, out there in the future? It might feel a little weird, but stick with it, as this is your chance to rewrite your life.

What did you write that isn't already in your life? Those items are now the focus for your life goals from this point on. What do you need to plan, and take action on now, for that eulogy to become true? Write them all down, decide on your first step, and then second, then third, then fourth.

This is all a waste of time unless you now do step one, then two, and so on. It's crucial you acknowledge and reward your progress along your journey. As you build up your track record of success with your one step at a time goals, then you can set bigger leaps which are achievable at a stretch. Keep focussing on what you do want, rather than what you don't. Most importantly, ditch the bitch and hang out with your best friend (you).

If you've just been reading, thinking, "Far out, that's a lot of writing", you are absolutely write, oops, right. However, if you prefer to make changes all on your own, then naturally there's more work involved. I want you to have the choice.

"You live the life of the person you believe you are."

Sue Lester

TIME TO CHANGE EXERCISE: GETTING PRESENT AND DE-STRESSED WITH A SENSES WALK

When your head is churning with what has been, what might be, or all those things to do, go for a Senses Walk. You'll come back calmer, thinking more clearly, and be so much more productive. You can turn it into fun and calming activity for your children too. By teaching them, you'll gain the benefits yourself immediately.

The key to de-stressing is to get out of your head and be fully present in the present, where you are safe. You can do this as a meditation-type exercise, in a quick few minutes sitting at your desk, or as a walk. I find the latter ideal as you are changing your state by changing your environment, you'll be pumping more oxygen to your brain and throughout your whole body, plus it's a chance to relax tight muscles and stiff body parts.

3:6 BREATHING

If you are feeling particularly upset or uptight, start by breathing – in through your nose for a count of three, and double that out through your mouth, counting to six in your own time and in your own way, so it's comfortable for you. Allow your breath out to feel like a warm waterfall of relaxation flowing all the way down your body … that's right.

Now, as you walk (or sit), choose a sense (sight, hearing, smell, touch, taste – only if you are having a meal!) to focus on for five to 10 minutes, then choose another for the next 10 minutes, and so on. For example, if you choose touch, notice how your clothes feel on your skin, the warmth of the sun, the breeze on your face, how your hair moves, the ground beneath your shoes, the touch of your feet in your shoes, the jewellery, watch or glasses touching your skin, the temperature and texture of the plants as you pass, and so on.

If you choose hearing, start by identifying or noticing sounds made by your body, then sounds close by, then sounds further away, then beyond that, and beyond that, casting your awareness further and further away. Or you could choose to focus on birds, or something of particular interest to you. If you are sitting in a room you can move your awareness eventually out into the universe, thereby turning it into a mediative process.

When you choose sight, I recommend you narrow that range of focus down so you don't go into overwhelm. You might choose to notice a particular colour, or shapes of leaves, or insects, or cars, or fences, or men etcetera. Play with the exercise, have fun exploring your world in the present, and notice how your breathing and your heartbeat calms, and your mind stills.

This exercise is also a great reminder that what we focus on is what we get. So changing your focus changes your results, and therefore how you feel. Leave the past behind you, where it belongs. Only go out into the future to clarify your destination. Focus on what you do want in life, rather than what you don't, take action, one step at a time, and notice the difference!

TIME TO CHANGE EXERCISE: MEGA TO DO LIST

This is another highly effective de-stressing exercise, though initially it may seem you'll increase your stress by highlighting exactly how much you do 'have' to do. It works because much of a feeling of overwhelm comes from your mental chatter reminding you not to forget this, wouldn't it be dreadful if you forgot that, what if this happens, what if that doesn't happen etcetera. You start to get anxious that you'll forget something important, but most of the chatter is repetitive small stuff about your daily routine or other people's wants. A large chunk isn't even real; it's just your imagination making up scary stories.

The idea of a mega to-do list is to dump it all out onto paper, that's right, vomit it all out. It helps even more if you can vomit into categories to ensure you get absolutely everything up and out. Include every single thing you have or should or want to do. Your list might include trimming your toe nails, petitioning the USA government to stop torture in custody, updating your website, advertising for a new sales manager, make the kids' hair appointment, and feeding the cat. Keep dumping it out until there is nothing left and you feel it's all out.

Now is actually the perfect time to create your mega to do list, otherwise this exercise will simply be something else to do. So pop your bookmark in here and put this book down.

• • • • •

Welcome back! Notice the silence in your head? Nice, isn't it?

The only thing you now need to remember is where your list is. Continue doing your daily, weekly, monthly and quarterly business planning in your diary, highlighting and focussing on your top three priorities. They will be much easier to identify now your head is clearer. Every so often you can review your mega list and tick what's been done if you wish; otherwise it has served its purpose and can be filed appropriately.

The penalty for not proactively managing your stress levels by effectively de-stressing regularly at all three levels is pain and dis-ease. Turn the page for more about those two penalties.

KEY POINTS

- » Three underlying causes of stress / overwhelm:
    1. Lack self-worth
    2. Lack self-trust
    3. Not living in the present
- » Three layers of de-stressing effectively:
    1. Physical
    2. Emotional
    3. Mindset
- » Practical strategies:
    1. Breathe 3:6
    2. Senses walk
    3. And what if it doesn't? How would that feel? (Quality Questions.)
    4. Acknowledge and reward
- » The only person you can change is yourself, however, there will be a rippleon effect to others.
- » The only person you need to forgive is yourself.

"Either you pay attention or you pay with pain."

Christopher Howard

NINE.
PAIN AND DIS-EASE

Disclaimer: I'm a firm believer in the power of the mind-body connection in creating and healing pain and dis-ease. I am not a medical practitioner or researcher, so am not qualified to give medical advice, nor replace the services of your own doctor or health professional. My beliefs have formed from my own health and life experiences, anecdotal evidence in my client practice, research on the placebo effect, and the works of others, including Dr Bruce Lipton, Dr Deepak Chopra, Dr John Demartini, Dr Ryke Geerd Hamer (in part), Dr Ian Gawler, Brandon Bays' Journey Work, and many more. The topic could easily fill a series of dedicated books, so this chapter was written with the intention of raising your awareness of how your own thoughts and emotions could be adversely impacting on your health, and to highlight ways that could support your own well-being journey.

• • • • •

The mind-body connection is a simple concept with complex manifestations. Personally, once my awareness was raised, particularly of the concept of secondary gain and the placebo effect, it was quite liberating and led me to regain more conscious control of my life. My intention is that your awareness will also be raised, and you'll be able to integrate the concepts and techniques in this chapter, improving your overall quality of life, including your relationships, both personal and professional.

For some, the idea that we can think ourselves sick or well is a ridiculous concept, yet even our language is filled with pointers. "She was paralysed with fear. I heard the news and felt sick to my stomach. My stomach knotted with fear, tension headaches and stress ulcers. The news was too much and he had a heart attack. The thought of public speaking made me break into a cold sweat, my hands shook, and I felt like throwing up. She gave up and died of a broken heart."

PLACEBO EFFECT

In some cultures, bone-pointing or curses were enough to ensure the demise of some hapless victim or wrongdoer. The collective belief that someone was so powerfully intent on punishing was enough to produce the desired result of illness, even death. Similarly, though with a different intended outcome, is the placebo effect. Researchers testing new medicines found approximately a third of the control group who were given sugar pills were likely to display an improvement in symptoms, and / or even the 'expected' side-effects of the real drug.

The likelihood of the placebo effect increased when the placebo looked genuine. Interestingly, injections were deemed more powerful than pills. Also important were the person's attitude to the potential success of the treatment, and the doctor-patient relationship. The higher the health care professional's credibility and connection with the patient, the better the results. Seemingly, many patients improved to keep their doctors happy, while a minority didn't so they could continue the regular contact.

Some of the theories attempting to explain the placebo effect include:

- **A change in behaviour** – the placebo may increase a person's motivation to take better care of themselves. Improved diet, regular exercise or rest may be responsible for the easing of their symptoms.

- **Altered perception** – the person's interpretation of their symptoms may change with the expectation of feeling better. For example, a sharp pain may be reinterpreted as an uncomfortable tingling.

- **Reduced anxiety** – taking the placebo and expecting to feel better may soothe the autonomic nervous system and reduce the levels of stress chemicals, such as adrenaline.

- **Brain chemicals** – placebos may trigger the release of the body's own natural painkillers, the brain chemicals (neurotransmitters) known as endorphins.

- **Altered brain state** – research indicates that the brain responds to an imagined scene in much the same way as it responds to an actual visualised scene. A placebo may help the brain to remember a time before the onset of symptoms, and then bring about physiological change. This theory is called 'remembered wellness'. (From http://www.betterhealth.vic.gov.au/bhcv2/bhcarticles.nsf/pages/Placebo_effect)

So if it works in one direction, to improve your health, then it also can work in the opposite, to make you ill. What you focus on, think about, feel about, you bring about. There's probably someone in your life who, no matter when you see her, is complaining about ill-health, while not taking any action to improve. Yet others beautifully hide terminal illnesses, determined to enjoy what life they have left, and making healthy choices every day to support that intention. When I started writing this book my mother was under palliative care, yet doggedly doing 10 laps of the carport, which runs the length of the house, twice a day, a kilometre in total. She actually exercised more than many supposedly healthy people I know.

SECONDARY GAIN

I was about six, I think, when I discovered that getting a headache that led to vomiting was the ideal way to avoid singing on stage in a Brownie (junior Girl Guides) concert. From there it was onwards and upwards, pardon the pun. I don't remember it being a conscious decision, but any time I was to be the centre of attention, including my own eighth birthday party, I seemed to get ill. Later, it became my response to high stress situations in the workplace too. I would be laid out for a day, vomiting from the pain, then take another couple of days before I felt strong again. When it stretched to three days of pain and vomiting, and seemingly linked in with my monthly cycle, I sought help from an NLP practitioner. His work certainly helped make it manageable, but it wasn't until I was studying NLP (Neuro Linguistic Programming) myself and learnt about secondary gain that the huge shift occurred.

Secondary gain is the benefit you derive from a seemingly negative event. I remember sitting in class, and it really was like someone turned on a bright light. I could suddenly see all the benefits I gained from investing in the pain episodes. I, first and foremost, avoided a potentially embarrassing or challenging public event. I received lots of attention and care from my poor mother who was mopping my forehead with a cool washer, coaxing me to drink flat lemonade and take headache tablets, emptying my sick bucket and worrying, as she continued to look after my brothers and dad. Later, it also gave my body time to rest and recharge with time-out from stressful work situations. I received care and attention from friends and boyfriends. The funny thing was that while I was processing my light bulb moment and getting excited about shedding the pain once and for all, another participant was standing up in class abusing the instructor for telling her she created her migraines and pain. She swore that there was absolutely zero benefit to her for having a migraine, and she'd take on anyone who insisted there was. The instructor shifted the participant's perspective to the point where she could accept that for some people, in some situations, secondary gain was a contributing factor to their painful headaches. I then volunteered my story as an example.

I decided to take conscious control and started working on a strategy to initially manage then free myself. First I changed the label from migraine to tension headache, as that was more accurate for me and reminded me of the underlying cause. I started paying attention. I stopped telling people when I had an episode, so that removed the TLC (tender loving care) from others. Instead, I started giving myself more TLC on a more regular basis. I used to wake up in the early hours of the morning with the headache underway, feeling powerless to stop it. I realised I actually always had a warning the night before – an out-of-sorts feeling in my body, and lots of tension. I worked out that if at the first sign I stopped and found a quiet spot with pencil and paper, I could negotiate a better solution with myself. (Yes, there I was, sitting in the corner talking with myself, and taking down the minutes!)

I started by thanking the pain for doing such a great job of getting my attention. I then confirmed I was now paying attention, so its job was done. It could stop now. Generally there was an instant reduction in pain, as muscles relaxed. Next I would close my eyes and ask, "What do I need to know about this?". And in response, start writing and writing and writing until I felt emptied, as if I had squeezed all of the pus out of the boil. Sometimes fears, some known and some unknown, came out. Sometimes it was simply that I needed to rest and de-stress. I would then negotiate with the part of me that created the pain.

For example, I would offer to take a sick day the next day to fully rest and recharge, in return for the pain disappearing completely. Or I might commit to a particular action in return for a pain-less body. I did find that if on waking up the next day feeling fine I merrily trotted off to work forgetting my commitment, I would get an even more savage headache in return. Sometimes during the writing part, instead of the pain easing more and more, I might get a stabbing pain. That was always a sign of an issue that needed further exploration, or was particularly significant. And remembering that you don't want to play in the pus you've cleaned out, nor do you want anyone else to, always destroy the paper completely after you've finished (burning it is quite satisfying, as is manually shredding it).

Ah, and in writing this it's occurred to me that my stomach's instant rejection of headache tablets and pain killers was a way of stopping me from missing the secondary gain.

Another example of the power of secondary gain, and the damage a values clash in a relationship can cause, is also from my own life. Yes, I did think about pretending it happened to someone else, but that would be slipping into the false ego, pretending everyone but me has 'issues'. And at some level, I'm a bit in awe of the power of my mind in this scenario. To set the scene, I was one of those kids at high school who knew exactly what they wanted to do with their lives, irritating to some, I know. I would move to Brisbane, study at the Mt Gravatt campus, become an early-childhood teacher, teach for three years, take a year's unpaid travel leave to explore Europe and Africa, return to teaching, study for my next degree part-time, marry in my late 20's, move back to my home town of Bundaberg, have two children and live happily ever after, spending Sundays enjoying family picnics at the beach. What a neat and safe plan, but as John Lennon sang, "Life is what happens when you are busy making other plans".

Firstly, I was tripped up by my love language; confusing orgasms with true love (remember the warning about kinaesthetic teenagers?). So I changed cities and study courses to be closer to 'love', and ended up walking down the aisle five days after my 20th birthday. I remember sitting in the hairdressers, having my wedding hair trial run, and reading a horoscope love compatibility article. I ran my finger down the page, lining up Sagittarius female with Cancer male, and read the exact words, "You've got to be joking!".

It changed my belief in the accuracy of such articles – it was so true! Lovely guy, but despite having matching love languages, the huge disparity in our values saw us on a trial separation only two and a half years later. The final crunch came when he said no to my European travel plans for us, as he preferred to put a deposit on a house and start a family straight away. Sensible perhaps, but I had been burning to get to England and Europe since I was five years old! I didn't want to have children and end up resenting them and hating him. And yes, I had very limiting beliefs that you couldn't travel overseas with children, and that your husband automatically tells the truth and learns to love whatever your interests are. So after winning my squash grand finals on my 23rd birthday, I packed up the remains of my married life and drove six hours home to my parents. Something clicked on that journey, and when I arrived I needed to be helped from the car. I was crippled over with throbbing pain. I still remember the doctor's grey eyes as he pronounced my life sentence, "Rheumatoid arthritis. You'll definitely be on pain killers for the rest of your life. You'll probably end up in a wheelchair".

I had felt like I was in a cage, madly flapping my wings against the bars. My husband had opened the door, and I hovered there, on the edge of freedom. The fears and self-doubts attacked and I tried to go back

PAIN AND DIS-EASE

into that safe, familiar cage, but I'd already been replaced. There was no room. So I froze and fell to the ground.

Just as my love language led me into the mess, so it rescued me, in the form of a lovely man who happened to love adventurous activities and travel, like me. I couldn't do that in a wheelchair, and he took my mind off the pain in a variety of ways. So the illness disappeared out of my system in a matter of weeks. In the years since it has threatened to return a few times, but now I recognise the warning signs of feeling scared and unloved. I choose to find other solutions so I can continue travelling and trekking all over the world, including the Himalayas, the Andes, Ruwenzori Mountains, New Zealand, Thailand and our own gorgeous Australian deserts.

Pain is your body's way of communicating that something isn't quite right and needs attention. Your unconscious mind uses your body to signal in the same way. Pay attention or pay with pain. Any pain over six weeks old generally has an emotional or psychological basis. You can do the writing and negotiation process described earlier in this chapter. For an even quicker answer, still your mind with some 3:6 breathing, as noted in earlier chapters. (Breathe in for three, out for six, at a pace that's comfortable for you. Allow each breath out to be a warm waterfall of relaxation flowing down your body.) Then simply place your hand on the painful part, and ask your unconscious, "What do I need to know from *here?*". Listen (it's not necessary to consciously think) for the answer. It might be simply one word, an image, or a whole story or movie. Of course, the next step is to take action, otherwise what's the point of doing the exercise?

Important: It is essential you provide alternative ways of getting the secondary gain benefits, otherwise you might simply replace one painful method with another. For example, voluntary time out, more self-care – including allowing yourself time out and to rest when needed, saying no more often, or a closer connection with others through pleasurable activities not rescuing your sick self.

Use this information to improve your other relationships and be aware of it in the workplace. If you only visit your mother when she is sick, you are training her that she needs to get sick every time she wants to see you. If your child is being bullied or struggling with school work, but their only escape is to be ill, then ill he or she will become. Likewise, if you are very busy with work commitments and other siblings, and the only quality time a child can get with you is by being ill, then of course they will be. Initially by pretending, but once you see through that genuine illness can manifest if needed. And on a lighter note, women, why do you think there is such a thing as 'man flu'?

REPRESSION

In earlier chapters you learnt how emotions have lessons attached, and how those emotions can build up in your system until you explode with anger, frustration or a flood of tears. Some have learnt it's safer or nicer to repress their emotions, festering away inside until they implode with dis-ease. A build-up of fear, from making up scary what if stories for the future, jams the adrenal system on. Churning stories over and over in your head works you into a frenzy, ready for battle or flight. Your stomach stops processing, you empty your bladder and bowels, and your heart is pumping blood hard to get more oxygen into the muscles that will need it most. Your whole body is tensed, ready for action.

The trouble is that your body is not designed to stay on high alert for more than a brief period of time, certainly not for years of stressful living. Your imagination, and how you perceive and process information through your senses and construct your own reality, affects your body's ability to function and heal itself as nature intended. That's why, as discussed in Chapter 8, it is crucial to de-stress at all three levels, physical, emotional and psychological. Once your body is back in equilibrium, it can maintain optimal functionality, regenerating itself at the cellular level.

When your mind is in equilibrium, fully in the present, it too functions at its optimum. You are no longer wasting energy on past regrets or future fears, tensioning your body and stretching its resources unnecessarily. You know what is most important to you at the deepest level, and live each day fulfilling those values. You are living on purpose, your purpose.

Not anyone else's idea of what your purpose should be. No matter what you do or don't do, some will approve and some will disapprove. Trying to please everyone and be liked by everyone ties you up in knots. I certainly don't expect everyone to like me, because I don't like everyone I meet. I can accept they have a different perspective to me and respect their right to that, but it doesn't mean I have to like them enough to spend any of my precious life in their company. Life is too short to spend with anyone who wants to change you to fit their idea of who you should be. Of course, if you don't know who you are, then you are fair game for anyone else who'd like to tell you.

If at this point you are telling yourself, "Aarrgh, that's the problem, I don't know who I am!".

Stop the B.S. (Translation for non-Australians: stop lying to yourself.)

Yes you do. Underneath all the layers of self-doubts, the lies, fears and other people's opinions, you do know. Drop those layers, step out and away, reveal the inner native you, and recognise who you are. All those beautiful characteristics you brought into the world as an innocent baby you still have. Plus you have all the courage, wisdom and resilience of all the lessons throughout your life to this point. Isn't it time to stop lying to yourself and others, and start being real? Your body will thank you for releasing all that tension of pretence. Yes, you may need support to do this, and to adjust others' expectations, but at least make the commitment to yourself to start today, one small step at a time.

I believe that state of being, living the life that really 'fits' you, with a congruent, unconscious blueprint™, is the true secret to eternal youthfulness. Note I used 'youthfulness' not 'youth'. I personally don't want to be a teenager with all that angst again, but I do want to retain the energy, wonder at the world, optimism and curiosity of youth. What about you?

EMOTIONAL PAIN: GRIEF

Over the past three years my interest in how people experience and process grief has moved from mostly professional to include a definite personal element. This is due to my family's journey with my mother's tumour (if our family used the 'C' word it would be called cancer) into palliative care, and my father-in-law's recent passing on March 19. I've noticed over the years how some are able to process the death of a loved one and move on with life, taking only the loving and fun memories forward. It can be easier when you can say a person has had a "good innings", a long life.

When a child or person dies earlier than expected, the pain of loss includes all the dreams and hopes for the future. Some people are able to take meaning from the death and use it to live their own lives more fully, sometimes actively helping others in similar situations or to ensure others don't die the same way. Sometimes living life fully as their child (whatever age) could have done – the fun, the adventure, the learning new skills and knowledge. They choose to be role models for those lucky enough to still be alive, reminding us to count our blessings and make the most of our lives. We don't know how long we have, so birthdays are to be celebrated.

An aside note here. If you struggle with feeling happy about having another birthday, or any anniversary for that matter, including wedding or job, then that's a flashing neon light you have regrets. If your life, marriage or career isn't what you expected or feel satisfied with, know that next year you will probably feel the same, if not worse.

If nothing changes, nothing changes.

It's your life, your choice (stepping into your personal power, At Cause here) to either do something about your unhappiness, or not. If not, then accept you don't have the ideal life, marriage or job. Accept you don't want to change (which is perfectly fine for you) and focus on the parts of your life you do enjoy. Everyone, including you, will likely feel so much better with that pressure off. Much energy is wasted futilely fighting against things you can't or won't change.

Others experiencing the death of a loved one seemingly cling to the pain, as if letting go in some way would mean they loved the person less. They set up shrines and shut down their lives. It is in these situations, and others involving the loss of careers, businesses and spouses through divorce, I observed the following:

LOSS + GUILT + RELIEF = GRIEF

In a recent training seminar participants were asked to share their stories of grief. It was very interesting, though not surprising, to hear how many clearly were consumed by guilt. Their pain of loss was intensified by guilt over what they said or didn't say, what they did or didn't do, what they could and couldn't control, including death itself. Every negative self-belief seemed to erupt out and beat them over the head with a blunt instrument. The deaths were confirmation of their unworthiness and their lack – in the end they just weren't enough.

However, underneath the tears and chest-beating lurked dark secrets, to their minds at least, if even acknowledged. That's where the relief element of the equation comes in. Life on earth is about balance. We live in magnetic fields, as demonstrated on a small scale with a pocket magnet under a piece of paper with iron filings on top. The magnetic fields are clearly visible then. You can't have a positive magnet nor can you have a negative magnet. Both positive and negative are integral to the whole. So for everything wonderful in your life, there is a downside. For example, when you said yes to your gorgeous husband, you said no to every other man (in theory, at least). You took on both the endearing and not so endearing (I believe snoring fits in here) qualities of your man. If you thought he was all positive, you were soon to be disappointed – as a balanced human he has his negative side too. As do you. Phew, what a relief for you – you don't have to be perfect either! Pressure off.

While trekking in Ladakh, northern India, recently and visiting nomadic camps and rural villages, it occurred to me how much of the stress in our modern lives comes from choice. In Australia the majority of the population have a mind-boggling range of choices every moment of our day – what we eat, what we clean ourselves with, what we dress in, the transport we choose, where and how we live, our careers, whom we marry or don't marry, iPhone or android, and so on.

Some become overwhelmed by choice because they know that saying yes to one means saying no to many more. They don't trust their own judgement, perhaps believe there is only one right choice, and so either procrastinate, rely on someone else's opinion, or choose then doubt that choice. Others stress by telling themselves they don't have a choice – they must stay in the relationship, the job, the living situation etcetera. Of course you have a choice. Yes, there are always consequences, but you do have choices every day on how you live your life. The level of satisfaction and contentment in your life is your responsibility, no one else's.

So in every death there are both positive and negative aspects. These will vary from person to person, depending on their own maps of reality as discussed in earlier chapters. It is easier to see the positive when an elderly person who has lived a rich and fulfilling life dies, so let's look at a more confronting scenario.

For example, a six-year-old girl dies. You can no doubt easily imagine many negative aspects of that, and perhaps empathise too, so I won't list examples of those. On the other side is the relief that she is out of pain, her organs helped other children live, the happy memories she created, the joy she brought into people's lives, the inspiration for living she gave, the relief that there will be no more hospital visits, medical bills, holidays delayed and 'normal' life put on hold, siblings pushed into the background, sleepless nights worrying and waiting, and stressful snapping at your spouse. Plus the relief the living hell is finally over.

You can see where guilt can come in with the relief, whether acknowledged or not. That relief doesn't make you or your partner bad people. It doesn't diminish the love you feel for your child in any way. You know she felt sad seeing you sad. It simply means you are human, with limited resources yet programmed to survive and thrive, just like everyone else. It's the denial rather than acceptance of the relief that generates more guilt and intensifies the grief. It seems the stronger the sense of relief, the stronger the subsequent guilt, the stronger the public grief.

If you are ready to accept both sides of the situation and to start releasing the grief by yourself, work through the following exercise. You may also wish to seek professional help, with a Demartini Method trained facilitator. For example, Dr John Demartini developed a highly effective process to clear the pain of grief in matter of hours, leaving you in a state of acceptance and love.

TIME TO CHANGE EXERCISE: GRIEF

For this exercise, divide a piece of paper into four columns. Down the left hand side of a page list all of the negative aspects of the death of the person, in other words, everything you miss and imagine you have lost.

Then, in column two, for each aspect, find who provides that to you now. For example, you might miss hugs. So who now has been hugging you more?

In column three, write the benefits of the new ways (for example the hugs from Person B). Write lots of benefits, at least 20, aiming for 50.

In column four, write the drawbacks if the person had lived, for example lesser connection with the person now giving the hugs. Once again, write as many as you can ferret out, at least 20 to get the best results.

You might find you start repeating some points as you move down the page, but that's fine, our lives are a web, not a single thread. Remember there is always a balance. Let go of those expectations of how you 'should' deal with death. Write them down. Keep adding to all four lists, letting your imagination run without censure. This is not the time for self-criticism – you've already over-achieved on that!

Keep writing until you reach the point where you totally feel 'it'. 'It' might be peace, silence, lightness, calm acceptance, love, but you'll know when you reach that point. All is okay.

If you suddenly feel guilty about feeling that all is okay, then you haven't fully completed the exercise. Go back and add in more and more points to all lists until you get that balanced feeling, or as suggested above, seek out professional facilitation.

Remember you can also use this exercise for the death of a marriage, business, career, good health or friendship.

> *"Life is too short to spend with anyone who wants to change you to fit their idea of who you should be."*
>
> *Sue Lester*

THE ROLE OF FORGIVENESS

Forgiveness can play a significant role in healing by reducing the stress and tension in your body that comes from reliving past pain, and mentally beating yourself and others up. In my early days of practice I used a forgiveness process I'd been taught which involved forgiving everyone who had ever looked sideways at you throughout your whole life. There's also a built in ego element there as when you say you forgive someone, you come from a superior position. You are forgiving someone for not living up to your values and standards. When a person doesn't feel in a superior position, they struggle with forgiveness as the power remains very much in the perpetrator's hands. Through my work over the years I've come to the conclusion that the only person you ever have to forgive is yourself.

No matter what you have or haven't done, or what others have or haven't done to you, the only person who controls the impact of that on your life, past, present and future, is you. Therefore, the only person you ever have to forgive is yourself.

What is the impact of the meaning you give to the event – does it make you a victim, dirty, wanton, unsafe, evil, pathetic, lost, labelled, incapable of happiness, unworthy of love, weak, deserving of abuse? How often do you replay the event? Do you take the muck from the past and spray it all over the future, feeling it happening over again? Are you using the past as an excuse to hide from life, to hide from your potential? Do you use it as emotional blackmail, your trump card for sympathy and getting your own way? (Ouch – did that question push your button?) How much of your personal power have you given and are continuing to give to that person or group? After all, no matter how traumatic the event, it is over now, and only exists in your memorised imagination. It only needs to be part of your identity if you wish it to be. When you allow a new person into your life, do you bring your trauma from the past into your new relationship, therefore into your present and future? If so, why? How do you want this new person to see you, to treat you?

An important part of letting it go is forgiving yourself for carrying it with you for so long, fertilising it and allowing it to grow – sprawling across the years of your life, choking the good times and blocking out the light.

Here is part of a powerful forgiveness process I use with clients. The full recording is available on my website. You can read the section below out aloud to yourself, with conviction, ensuring you sound like you mean the words. Otherwise, please don't bother as you'll do more harm than good.

"The only person you ever have to forgive is yourself."

Sue Lester

# TIME TO CHANGE EXERCISE: SELF-FORGIVENESS PROCESS

To start, find yourself a quiet place and begin with breathing 3:6 (in for a count of three, out for a count of six, so it's comfortable for you), feeling that warm waterfall of relaxation with every breath out. Then read, ideally out aloud, walking around, to engage more senses and really embody this loving message to yourself.

I acknowledge I've increased the pain in my life by bringing my past into my present, and projecting it out into the future.

I'm ready now to reclaim my personal power.

I'm ready to forgive myself completely in every version of myself I've been in the past, present and future.

I am ready to move forward in my life, free from restrictions and limitations.

I forgive myself for all the times I said yes, when I should have said no.

I forgive myself for all the times I said no, when I should have said yes.

I forgive myself for speaking up when I should have remained silent.

I forgive myself for remaining silent when I should have spoken up.

I forgive myself for all the times I lied, cheated, stole and killed living creatures, ideas and emotions.

I forgive myself for all the times I was mean, cruel, spiteful, petty and deceitful to myself and others.

I forgive myself for all the times I didn't believe in myself, and for all the times I believed other peoples' opinions of me.

I forgive myself for all the times I withheld love from myself and others, whether from fear, ignorance or spite.

I forgive myself for all the times I made unhealthy choices, self-sabotaged and denied my true worth.

I forgive myself for all the times I told myself I wasn't enough.

I forgive myself for all the times I told myself I was undeserving. I know now I always was and always will be worthy of love.

I forgive myself for all the times I didn't allow myself to learn, expecting immediate mastery, and giving up when that wasn't humanly possible.

I forgive myself for all the goals I set then blocked myself from achieving.

I forgive myself for wasting my life living in the past with regrets and in the future with fear.

I forgive myself for comparing myself unfavourably and unfairly to others.

I forgive myself for being human, not perfect.

I now know all I have to do is to be me, the best me I can be.

All is well, I am loved.

What is your colour for forgiveness? Then imagine that colour flooding your body, soaking into every cell and the space between your cells, from the tip of your head to the tip of your fingers to the tip of your toes.

Ideally you will be feeling much lighter now. If not, then what self-belief are you clinging to, what story are you telling yourself about yourself that is still causing pain? As long as you believe you deserve to suffer, you will.

FOCUS ON GOOD HEALTH

Once you clarify and tune into (turn on your Reticular Activating System) the healthy choices you want, then daily choices become much easier. The more you focus on what you do want, how good it feels and the multitude of ways those healthy choices will fulfil your other life goals, the easier it is to succeed. Your perceived lack of will-power will stop weighing heavily on your mind. Read on for more about this.

KEY POINTS

- » The Placebo Effect is evidence of the strong mind-body connection in creating and healing dis-ease and pain.
- » Secondary gain is the underlying benefit of having an apparently negative issue.
- » The secondary gain must be identified and replaced with an alternative before true healing occurs.
- » Pain is your body's way of communicating that something is not right and needs attention.
- » Repressing strong emotion causes dis-ease in your body.
- » Loss + Guilt + Relief = Grief
- » Balancing out the positives and negatives of a death will give you peace of mind.
- » You always have a choice; you just might not like the consequences.
- » Life is too short to spend with someone who wants to change you to suit them.
- » The only person you ever need to forgive is yourself.

PAIN AND DIS-EASE

*"You can't stop the waves,
but you can learn how to surf."*

Unknown

TEN.

WEIGHING HEAVILY IN YOUR MIND

Did you realise that food accounts for a high percentage of deaths in the world every year? Deaths from the consequences of too much, too little, or poorly prepared food, and the diseases that follow. You can see it on the streets, and in hospitals, both in patients and sadly in the staff too. While paying hospital visits recently I was shocked by how many very overweight nurses and support staff there were, working unhealthily long shifts caring for patients suffering from the impact of unhealthy lifestyle choices. Ironic, isn't it? Chances are if you are reading this you're in the minority of the world population that is surrounded by an abundance of food, nourishing and otherwise. You know that portion control, healthy food / drink choices and regular exercise can keep you trim and healthy, yet do you find yourself struggling in a cycle of diets and over-indulgence? Do you catch yourself sabotaging your best efforts? Very likely there are deeper level (unconscious) reasons for this. Through my work with a wide range of people over the years, I've found these fall into three overlapping categories: self protection, self-abuse, and family fat.

Once the deeper level reasons are discovered, it is so much easier to understand your behaviour and make those changes you want to see. Please read the following pages slowly, with an open mind, paying particular attention to those points which 'push your button'. There is a clue there for you. Many apply equally to men, and you may recognise some traits starting in your children. As always, awareness is the first key to change. It's important your awareness comes from the observer position, not judging or criticising or blaming, nor playing the helpless victim. Instead you are simply becoming aware of what is happening at that deeper level, so you can make changes if you wish.

After exploring each of the three categories we'll look at what you can do differently now.

SELF-PROTECTION

In this category is the underlying belief that being overweight is sexually unattractive and therefore will keep her safe from unwanted advances. This is common in females who have been sexually abused. It is also common in females who have developed physically before they could emotionally deal with the attention given to their budding breasts and curves. That attention could be in the form of taunting school boys, or men whose comments, looks and touches are confusing and threatening. Sometimes the trigger is simply growing up with stories of attractive women 'asking for it', with the insinuation that curvy women deserve to be raped. The fat is seen to cover dangerous curves.

Conversely, rather than being used as an invisibility cloak, excess fat is also a way of making yourself look bigger and less vulnerable. Extra body weight can be a way of making yourself more visible, so you and your needs won't be overlooked in your chaotic world. Body fat can also literally be a protective barrier to absorb the impact of physical abuse.

Over eating can be an act of defiance, for example, "You can control the rest of my life but not what I eat or how I look". This is a factor in cases of anorexia nervosa, which also fits into the self-abuse category. A fat body can be used as an overt excuse for not being in a relationship. However, there are millions of overweight people in happy relationships across the world, so that excuse is a sign of an underlying fear of intimacy and / or low self-worth. If you don't love yourself, perhaps because you felt your parents didn't love you so therefore you were unlovable, you won't believe that anyone else can either. It's only with the wisdom of hindsight as adults we can look back and understand that the issue was the parents' lack of personal resources, not that the child was unlovable. The ensuing loneliness leads to comfort eating which perpetuates the cycle.

Comfort eating is to fill a hole in the soul. The key is to identify what is needed to fill that hole, and food, not even chocolate alas, is never the answer. (Did you realise 'desserts' is 'stressed' spelt backwards?) Self- love, connection to others, and a sense of belonging are more likely answers. The next step is to identify all the different ways you can bring those into your life, and then start taking action on them. Have that bubble bath, make that telephone call, and ditch the bitch (negative self-talk).

But wait, there are even more benefits to excess weight. Your extra body fat can be an excuse not to take risks and fully live life. You can't fit into that kayak, or walk up that hill, or apply for that better job, or post your photo on that online dating site. Later, when your long suffering joints give out on you, your legs swell until you can barely walk and the diseases kick in, it can make you dependent on others, binding those with obligations to care for you. Is this your future, or perhaps you see this in an older relative?

Those 'spare tyres' can be an unattractive buffer when not wanting sex within a relationship, such as after the birth of a child or as a punishment for being unfaithful or not living up to childhood fantasies of Prince Charming and living happily ever after in the palace. It can be a protective barrier to conception and all the associated deep level fears that come with bringing a baby into the world.

How are you doing? Did you notice any tender or sore points? What ah-ha moments did you have about others in your life?

SELF-ABUSE

There can be an overlap between self-protection and self-abuse for an individual as although initially the excess weight was for protection, the overeating can then morph into self-abuse for some. Excess weight, the failure of diets, not sticking to gym schedules etcetera become confirmation of their own unworthiness, and proof of being a failure. The underlying, disempowering self-beliefs are of being not enough, unlovable or unworthy of love, and a failure.

The excess body fat becomes an excuse not to actively pursue dreams or relationships which would disprove those beliefs. What if you met someone who saw different facets of you, all your wonders, and fell in love with you? Part of you instinctively doesn't trust him, because obviously his judgement is out, or he's lying to you, because you know you're not lovable and he'll eventually discover that and leave. Just like the others. It's safer not to go there in the first place, isn't it? (Sound familiar, for you or others?)

Overeating 'unconsciously' creates disease to shorten an unhappy life. Otherwise why, when all of the medical research is there to show the damage done to our bodies, the heart disease statistics, the consequences of diabetes and so much more, do people still choose to over eat fast food and junk food? If you have you ever reached for something particularly fatty or loaded with sugar, paused, then said, "Ah, what the hell!" you'll understand what I'm saying.

Also in this category is the woman who stays with a possessive partner who encourages overeating so she won't be attractive to others, thereby reducing the risk that she will leave the relationship. At some level she doesn't believe she is good enough for a better man, or even that another man would even look at her. For example, that woman was me in the 1990's. Whenever I scraped up enough self-love to exercise in the morning and cook healthier food, he would come home from the confectionary warehouse with, literally, two shopping bags full of sugary death and potato chips. He'd suddenly decide he needed to eat takeaway pizza (thick crust double cheese) or chicken and chips, four nights a week. Fortunately, he left for work quite early, so I could exercise without his interference. Each night coming home from work I'd look up at the kitchen window, and if the light was on I'd feel sick in my stomach because it meant he was home already.

I spent eight years, the last of my good breeding years, in that abusive relationship because what if I couldn't find another man who might want children with me? Even at the end, when I knew I was in physical danger if I stayed and had put my escape plan in place, I still spent a day pacing up and down the Sandgate foreshore reassuring myself that he wasn't the last man on earth that would want me. It took me only three months to shed 10 kilos of excess fat and get fit enough to go trekking with the Outback Camel Company in our beautiful Australian deserts. But it took another three years before I felt healed enough to date again. If only I'd known more about NLP and looked for professional help, I would have healed and moved on much faster.

As already mentioned, anorexia nervosa is both self-protection in the form of taking control of the family dynamics, and also a form of self-abuse at the other end of the spectrum. The topic is a whole book in itself, so I am simply raising the flag of awareness here. Likewise, bulimia, the gorging and then purging of food by vomiting or laxatives, is out of the scope of this text. It is a very controlled form of self-abuse.

For some, their low self-esteem and need to punish themselves comes from being labelled 'fat' or 'plump' or 'dumpy' as a child, particularly if that labelling was done by parents.

FAMILY FAT

This broad category covers the influence of our family on our eating habits and identity. It naturally overlaps with self-protection and self-abuse, as mentioned above.

For some it is simply that they have been fed fat food from in the womb throughout their whole lives. How and what a woman eats, exercises, handles stress, laughs and plays during pregnancy are lessons being passed on. So if you want your children to eat their greens, eat lots yourself, with pleasure, while pregnant! If you're resentful or your stomach is contracting, that message will be passed on too.

These children can be born with excess fat and will grow up being surrounded by overweight people who have patterned that behaviour. Their tastebuds are used to high salt and high sugar foods, and certain textures. They haven't learnt to cook healthy options, and have lifestyle habits centred on fast and snack food, drinking soft drinks, juice, flavoured milk or alcohol instead of water. A hug from a slim person might not feel as loving as one from a plump person, if that's what you are used to. As we choose partners with similar interests and values, chances are you will choose someone also overweight without even noticing.

Punishment and reward are dealt in food. Saying "No" to a (or another) piece of the cake your mother made becomes a rejection of her love. Dieting and talking about and trying the latest wonder diets is acceptable as long as you don't succeed, because if you succeed, you will no longer fit in as well. You will look different, act different and not join in the feasting in quite the same way. You will also be saying, even without words, "If I can do it, so can you". And that will be an unwelcome message for some family and friends, while others will be encouraged and follow your lead. It takes strong self-belief and commitment to go against family values, but once you set the path, it's easier for others, especially the next generation, to follow.

Similar patterns follow in smoking families, though with anti-smoking campaigns in Australian schools which make the health consequences of smoking very clear, children are more likely to influence their parents' behaviour. There's nothing like seeing your child in anxious tears every time you light up to shift your values. Feeding yourself a slab of chocolate cake won't generate the same response, even though the consequences can be as life threatening over time.

As you know, regular exercise is an essential component of life, not only for releasing excess weight, but most importantly for maintenance of a healthy body and clear mind. As the saying goes, "Use it or lose it". As discussed in Chapter 8, De-stress For Success, regular exercise is invaluable for stress management. If you grew up racing around the yard playing tiggy, climbing trees, riding your bicycle for independence and enjoying school sport, you have the advantage of a happy association with exercise. However, people who have grown up overweight have often never experienced any pleasurable physical activity as it has always been painful, uncomfortable or humiliating and never fun. They may or may not have self-protection or self-abuse unconscious beliefs too.

Please note, when I'm using the word 'exercise' I'm talking about movement – whether formally allocated time such as gym, sport, swimming laps etcetera, or simple choices such as walking up the stairs instead of using the escalator, physical gardening, and actively playing with your kids and pets rather than just watching them have all the fun.

The concept of exercise as we know it is a modern invention to counteract the effects of technology and those labour-saving devices. Now you no longer have to spend hours doing the laundry by hand, boiling heavy sheets in the copper, then hanging them (wringing wet) out to dry, you need to go to an exercise class and lift weights. As you drive a car rather than walk or ride your bike to work and the shops, you need to go to the gym to do a spin-class or walk on the treadmill instead. Or not, and there is the problem. Remember, you don't need to wear lycra, as long as you are finding lots of ways of moving and using different muscles in your daily routine.

Family fat is not an excuse or a cop-out for not now choosing to have a healthy body. Your body is continuously renewing and regrowing itself, so it is never too late, apart from when you're dead. Imagine your last thought being, "I wish I had...".

Actually, if you knew you were going to die in a few minutes, how would you finish this sentence?

"I wish I had _____

_____."

Right now, as I type, mine would be, "I wish I had cleared my fears sooner and published this book already!".

Those in this family fat category will simply need to spend more time re-educating themselves, their tastebuds and bodies. Yes it will take commitment and time, but considering you are improving the quality of the rest of your life, and avoiding the expense and pain of illness, could it be worth it? Are you worth committing to? Experts like nutritionist Lisa Cutforth, www.ivegotlife.com.au, who also understand the role of the mind in healthy weight, are worth their weight in gold.

Looking closely at how and what health problems and limited life choices you are passing on to your children can be a kick-start motivator. Note: beating yourself up for being a terrible mother and reaching for a consoling chocolate biscuit is missing the point. Feeling guilty about past actions is a disempowering waste of energy. The past is past, but now that you do have awareness, what are you choosing to do differently now? (If you choose to do nothing, and then feel free to bring on the guilt, load up that self-abuse ... but that would be sad for those you love, wouldn't it? Aren't you more than that?)

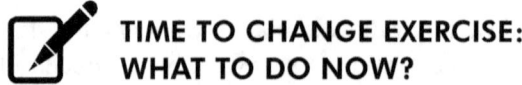# TIME TO CHANGE EXERCISE: WHAT TO DO NOW?

If you are overweight and still reading, congratulations! Take a moment now to grab a pen and some paper, or make notes in this book. Writing helps crystallise your learning and reduces the mental white noise because you can only think of one thing at a time while you are physically writing.

So, I recommend you write down what points stirred you up the most, and consider why. Why did that comment hurt, or bring up anger?

_____
_____
_____

What beliefs about yourself and your family were challenged?

_____
_____
_____

Which of the three categories do you fit into? How do you know?

_____
_____
_____

Knowing now that a healthy body is a combination of mental and emotional health, plus healthy lifestyle choices, write down what you would like to change.

_____
_____
_____

What are the benefits of that change? How will you feel? What will be different in your life?

_____

_____

_____

Consider and write down what next steps you could take. Do a brainstorm.

_____

_____

_____

Choose just one to start; knowing that one small, successful change is far more valuable than a large change not achieved. Progress is simply one step after another towards your desire.

_____

_____

_____

What do you need to do to support your move forward? For example, allocate time, book a babysitter, stock the pantry and fridge with only healthy choices, get help with self-esteem issues etcetera.

_____

_____

_____

Does your unconscious blueprint™ need to be changed to reflect a healthy body? What would change?

___

___

___

Who can best help you succeed?

___

___

___

Sometimes bringing an issue to light is enough to dissolve it, however, if the underlying emotional issue has been present for a lengthy time you will find it easier to clear with the help of a trained NLP practitioner or coach. Once you forgive yourself and start practising self-love, you'll find it so much easier to make loving choices for yourself. Remember, you are saying "No" to chocolate cake from love, not to punish yourself. Every time you say "No Thanks" to unhealthy options, you are really saying "Yes" to yourself with love.

Before we move on, here's a powerful language re-programming tip for you.

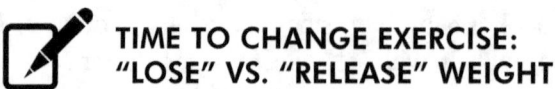
TIME TO CHANGE EXERCISE: "LOSE" VS. "RELEASE" WEIGHT

If you 'lose' something, what do you do? Go looking for it, right?

And how do you feel about losing something? Anxious, frustrated, worried, guilty and annoyed?

Our unconscious mind associates the word 'lose' and 'loser' with negative connotations, so 'losing' weight is also negative at that deeper level. And who wants to be the biggest loser in the country?

Call it 'releasing weight' and notice the difference in how that feels. 'Releasing' is positive as it implies choice and free will. There's also no expectation to see it again!

Imagine, if you wish, releasing all those little blobs of fat back into the wild, letting them run free to settle elsewhere ..."Whee!"

Remember!

You are aiming for your healthy body, not someone else's. Or worse, some airbrushed image in the media that is physically impossible to attain. We are all shapes, sizes and colours, which makes the world a rich tapestry, rather than a boring pattern of sameness. Aim for the healthiest version your body can be. The curves and weight of muscle are part of a healthy body.

Be reassured that anything can be changed for good, if that's what your heart desires.

Know that no matter what you may or may not have done in the past, you always were and always will be worthy of love. In the next chapter we continue exploring the impact of unconscious programming, including the power of language.

KEY POINTS

- » There can be underlying emotional and psychological reasons for excess weight.
- » Self-protection provides a physical and emotional buffer.
- » Self-abuse confirms own negative self-identity.
- » Family fat – generational poor habits and emotional connection to food.
- » Remember 'exercise' is movement. Use it or lose it.
- » Aim for the healthiest version of your body, not someone else's.
- » Utilise the power of language with encouraging self-talk, and 'release' your excess weight.

WEIGHING HEAVILY IN YOUR MIND

"A happy life is just a string of happy moments. But most people don't allow the happy moments, because they're so busy trying to get a happy life."

Abraham-Hicks

ELEVEN.
ARE YOU UNCONSCIOUSLY BLOCKING CONCEPTION?

This chapter can be read in two ways, either as its original intention, a resource for unexplained infertility, or as a metaphor for the conception of an idea or a goal, whether in business or personal life. Where are unconscious fears and beliefs blocking you?

You and your partner have been doing all the 'right' things to promote conception, including eating and drinking healthily, practitioner herbal supplements, exercising moderately (strenuous exercise can disrupt the female cycle and cook his sperm), detoxifying your environment and your bodies (including clearing heavy metals and getting sperm in optimum fitness), de-stressing and de-cluttering your lives, and having lots of lovely, orgasmic sex, particularly around ovulation. Phew, sounds like hard work! Actually, all those factors should be 'normal' in a healthy lifestyle, and are less significant when both are in the prime breeding age. Squeezing a child into a very busy lifestyle later in life necessitates extra conscious preparation.

This last point about sex gets overlooked surprisingly often in busy stressful modern lives, and of course, the pressure to perform can be a real turn off. Few men want to feel like a sperm factory. If you are having sexual intercourse only once a week, or less, naturally you're decreasing your odds of conceiving dramatically. You'll never to learn to play the piano well if you only practice weekly. Assuming your sex life isn't the issue, but it's been more than 12 months since you decided the time was right – there's no physical reason not to but you still haven't conceived, so what else might be happening? That's where the unconscious preparation comes into play.

Statistics vary, but approximately one in six Australian couples are labeled 'infertile', that is, haven't conceived within 12 months of regular, unprotected sex, and out of those, for roughly 10 per cent there is no physical reason not to conceive. You aren't alone!

The power of the mind over the body is increasingly well-documented. If you have chosen to delay parenthood because of career, lifestyle or relationships issues, then your crew (aka unconscious mind) has already collated a whole list of reasons why having a baby is not a great idea. You've put the brakes on so many times they are stuck, and there's a fear of what might happen if the free-wheeling starts. Some days the message is "yes", some days "maybe not", and some days "thank goodness not"! There's still that agony of what if we regret not having a baby, and what if we regret having one? While those thoughts churn on top of your daily stresses, your body will feel tense most of the time.

Beyond that is the stage where the sight of a baby or a pregnant woman upsets you. Particularly painful if it is someone you know or someone you see in the street whom you think doesn't deserve to have a baby. The painful thoughts and all the feelings of sadness, anger at the unfairness, guilt and fear well up. That's a sign you've trained your body to associate babies with pain, and of course, pain is something we instinctively avoid.

Fortunately it's also possible to clear that excess negative emotion out of your system and to re-train your mind and body, anchoring in a powerful positive response to babies and pregnancy. That response you used to have. Or perhaps you've never had that strong maternal instinct, and it is more of a logical decision for you. Some women, and men, don't feel strongly positive about babies until they hold their own. Some not even then, and it's only when the child is old enough to interact the connection is felt. Note that not bonding with your newborn can also be a sign of post-natal depression so please seek professional support sooner rather than later.

Let's explore that negative anchoring concept more. Have you ever wanted something so badly that the sight or thought of someone else having it made you furious, sick to the stomach or tearful? Maybe it's that promotion, that partner, that baby? Desire can motivate us, but taken to the extreme it works in reverse, driving away what we most want, spiraling us down into despair. This may sound overly dramatic for those who haven't experienced this or know someone who has. However, I've worked with many clients experiencing this, and I know many of you will totally relate to what I'm saying.

You may have heard of The Law of Attraction, so perhaps feel that since you want something so badly, it has to come to you. The key, of course, is how you feel when you think about what you desire and what actions you take. How you feel about a goal anchors into your body, so after repetition of desire, simply the sight, sound, mention or thought of the goal (or similar) will immediately generate the same response in your body. The idea is that you are filling your body with positive sensations, so psychologically and physiologically you program yourself that this goal is a very good thing for you. The bonus is that you are certainly more likely to achieve your goal / desire, and most importantly, your journey will be a pleasant, positive experience.

The opposite works the same way. If you continually experience strong, negative emotions when you think of your desire, for example, anger, jealousy, frustration, sadness, fear and guilt, you will anchor those into your body. The result is you'll associate your goal with pain, and unconsciously strive to avoid achieving it. So, you not only miss your desire, you have a miserable journey grabbing at something you always keep out of reach, in order to protect yourself from the pain.

For example, this means that if you are conceiving, on IVF or not, yet the sight of someone else's baby or a pregnant woman sets off a negative emotional chain reaction, you are training your body that baby = pain and pregnancy = pain. And, of course, we are programmed at a survival level to instinctively avoid pain. You need to train your body to believe that baby = love, and pregnancy is a highly desirable state. You may need to collapse your negative baby and pregnancy anchors (easily done using Neuro Linguistic Programming).

Next, you need to layer in a new positive anchor by flooding your body with warm, loving, protective, happy feelings at every opportunity. This will involve stepping out of your own 'stuff' and looking at a baby with new eyes, marveling at it as the innocent, unique and miraculous being it is. Touching, holding, smelling and looking at it lovingly will all generate the positive anchoring in your body. Likewise, the pregnant woman you see is also a miracle on her own journey. She's not chosen to conceive to hurt you, and by ascribing that meaning in your body you hurt yourself more than anyone else could.

Similarly, if you are jealous of another's good fortune, for example, a promotion or successful business, you are anchoring in that success = pain, or wealth = pain. You are also closing off opportunities to share that good fortune. If you were expanding your business and looking to head-hunt a former colleague, would you consider the one who had sour grapes, or the one who was generous of spirit and genuinely pleased at your success? Take a moment to look at a desire you haven't yet achieved, and ask yourself what you are anchoring in, and whether you are helping or hindering your chance of success. Look at ways you can turn your attitude and behaviour around to serve your purpose better. What aspect can you focus on, that will serve you better?

Typically that intense level of negative response comes after years of disappointment, so what could be happening to block conception before that point?

The key is in how we learn to survive in our world. Every second of the day and night our senses are bombarded with enormous amounts of information. To enable us to function effectively, our brains have developed filters which delete, distort or generalise the information into manageable chunks. Our filters start developing in the womb, and particularly in the Imprint Period, birth to seven years old, we are like little sponges, soaking up all the experiences without the benefit of a developed critical faculty.

Our filters include our values, beliefs, decisions, memories, attitudes and more, and whatever information makes it through the filters becomes part of our individual Map Of Reality, that is, how each of us uniquely interprets the world around us. How we interpret the world, both consciously and unconsciously, determines our emotional state which impacts on our physiology which impacts our behavior and consequently the results we get. Our unconscious blueprint™ is formed along the way.

So how does this relate to conception? Our experiences, the stories we hear, the images we see, our (mis)interpretations, and our feelings as we grow up are stored a deep unconscious level, but nevertheless form our filters and determine our behaviour. For example, a two-year-old playing near her mother and aunt could hear a horror birth story which imprints a deep level belief that having a baby is a terrifying, agonising and dangerous experience to be avoided at all costs.

Over the years, this belief is re-enforced by media images and other anecdotal stories. How many birth scenes have you seen on TV or in movies that involve a calm, inwardly-focused woman listening to and moving her body to assist her baby birth? None? How about flat on her back, swearing and screaming? Perhaps dying in pools of blood? Little wonder our bodies tense with fear at the thought of birthing. Please be alert for little girls watching such images, and reassure them it isn't real, just acting, and that bringing a baby into the world doesn't have to be like that.

Fortunately, with the advent of YouTube, if you are wishing to conceive you can watch as many hypno birthing and positive birthing video clips as you can find. I strongly recommend you read Marie Mongan's book, *Hypno Birthing the Mongan Method*. The women's stories open up a whole new world of birthing possibilities, and will help imprint a positive alternative for you. Some editions also include a meditation CD to connect you with your unborn child, and train your body to relax. You don't need to be pregnant or female to benefit. Then when you are pregnant, I strongly recommend you and your partner attend hypno birthing or similar classes as part of your parenting preparation. Dr Sarah J. Buckley's book, *Gentle Birth, Gentle Mothering*, is another must-read.

If you have unconscious blocks to conception, what do you think they might be? In my personal journey I discovered my blocks were that, "Children are a sacrifice and the end of choice. You can't travel overseas with children. Birth is always hours of screaming agony". Plus I had a mysterious fear of my waters breaking in a supermarket aisle! I've no idea where that one came from – a conversation I overheard as a small child, perhaps?

TIME TO CHANGE EXERCISE: IDENTIFYING UNDERLYING BELIEFS

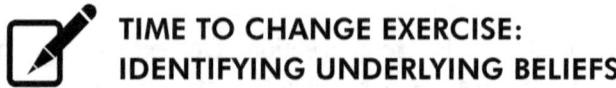

Here is a selection of other beliefs I've helped my clients uncover and clear, some of which may resonate with you. Bear in mind we can hold beliefs unconsciously that our adult conscious mind dismisses as nonsense. Read through slowly, considering each and noticing which give you the strongest reaction.

"A baby means being stuck at home, bored and boring."

"Birth involves more pain than I could bear."

"Husbands are always unfaithful to pregnant wives."

"I'll end up being just like my mother."

"I'm not grown up enough to be a parent." (Definitely check your unconscious blueprint™ if this resonates.)

"A baby means the end of my career."

"Pregnant women are fat and ugly."

"I don't trust my partner."

"I can't protect my child from being abused like I was."

"I don't deserve a child."

"We can't afford a baby."

"A baby is the end of freedom and fun."

"I'll lose my identity and just be a mum."

"Giving birth means the end of great sex – I'll be over-stretched and fat."

"A baby means my mother-in-law will practically move in with us and really take over."

"My partner works long hours and does nothing around the house now, so it'd be like being a single mum."

"Old mothers have deformed babies."

"Babies get sick and die, and that hurts more than I could bear."
"The world is an unsafe place for children."
"I'm not strong enough to protect my children."
"My abused body is dirty and not a fit place to nurture an innocent child."
"I'd make a terrible parent because I'm too selfish."

Which resonated most with you? What others have you heard yourself say? What have you learnt about yourself and your journey forward?

Here are two methods you can use for greater self-awareness, and for decision making.

 TIME TO CHANGE EXERCISE: MIND MAPPING

Fortunately, what you can identify you can change, particularly with the right mindset reprogramming techniques. An effective exercise you can do at home to further identify underlying blocks is mind mapping. It has conventionally been used as a creative brain-storming technique and I find it an invaluable tool for clients to use at home to raise greater self-awareness between sessions. And yes, you can use this to explore unconscious blocks to any life or business goal. I've also used it to as a communication tool with troubled but silent teenagers.

You'll need a quiet place, paper, and a selection of coloured pens. Start by drawing a smallish circle in the middle of your page. Write your focus word inside, for example baby. Choose a life area to start, for example career, relationship, self, health or finances etcetera. Draw a long branch from the circle and label it. Relax and allow your mind to explore every nook and cranny of the connection between baby and career, for example. Write each train of thought down on a separate 'twig' off the branch. Circle any 'Aha' thoughts as you go, or write them on a separate piece of paper for further action.

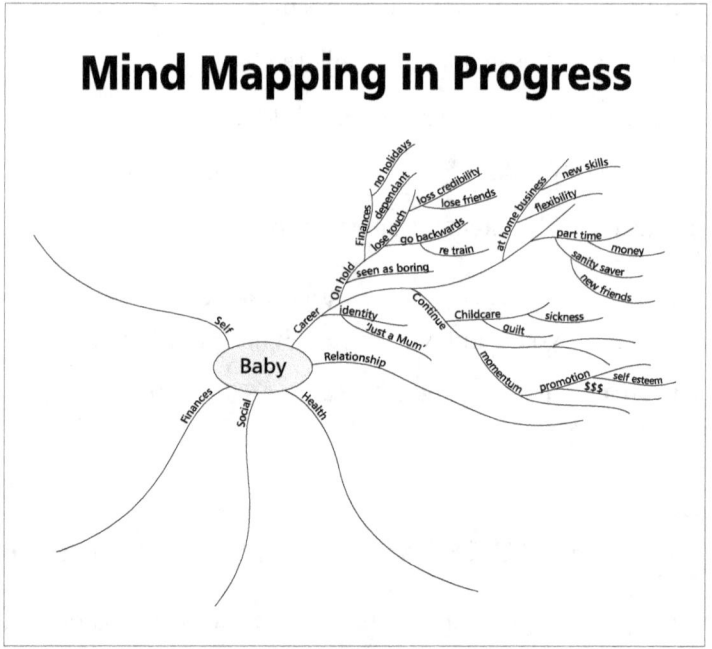

Complete each life area the same way, in a different colour, and you could be surprised at what you uncover. It's important to include both positive and negative thoughts and not to censure yourself in any way – it's only for your eyes. An uncomfortable thought is a significant clue, so let it out without judging. Write it down and explore it further.

Ideally, your partner will also do one for him / herself, and then you can share and explore your discoveries together, if you wish. Choose a time when you are both relaxed and comfortable to do this. If your partner resists doing his own, you can still benefit from sharing and discussing yours. Remember, it's not about blame or criticism. It's simply exploring and sharing what's happening for you beneath the surface. It is what it is, and now you are aware you have the option to change what no longer serves you.

For example, a client who had been through years of disappointment and six unsuccessful IVF cycles did this exercise and was surprised that, "Having a baby would make me bored and boring" came up. Another discovered she was worried about losing the respect and connection with her current career-orientated social circle. "Life sentence" popped up for another.

For even greater clarity, and for any important decisions that have been identified, the following can be very useful.

TIME TO CHANGE EXERCISE: CARTESIAN LOGIC

This exercise is ideal for decision making as it enables you to walk around a decision, revealing the pros and cons across all areas of your life. In doing so, it can reveal previously unconscious points of resistance or fear. That feature makes it an invaluable tool for couples making significant decisions. Its application within the workplace, particularly during cultural or structural changes, can make transition much smoother as resistance can be identified and resolved.

The process involves answering four deceptively simple questions. These quantum linguistic questions are also working at the deeper unconscious level. For each question, consider it fully across every area of your life and write the answers down. For example, what will the impact be on you personally, your self-esteem, health, wealth, career or business, relationships, children, living arrangements, transport, education / training, holiday plans, pets, friendships, social life, sex life etcetera?

Write down whatever pops into your mind, without censuring, and including positive, negative and neutral points. This is not the time to focus on positive thinking like one client did. She discovered that if you only write down the positive aspects all options look wonderful, which defeats the purpose of the exercise. No matter what option you ultimately choose, there will always be a downside, simply because yes to one automatically means no to others.

By considering each question fully across all areas of your life, by the end of the exercise you will have a much clearer perspective on which decision is best for you, and most importantly, why. This frees you up to move confidently forward on your path, not someone else's.

Here are the questions:

1. (Positive Positive) What will happen if you do _____?
(Have a baby, resign, adopt a kitten, hire a manager, move to Gympie etcetera.)

2. (Positive Negative) What will happen if you don't _____?

3. (Negative Positive) What won't happen if you do _____?

4. (Negative Negative) What won't happen if you don't _____?

Once you've uncovered some potentials blocks you'll need to consider what your next steps are to clear them or change them into something more empowering.

Is it something you can resolve by consciously self-correcting or researching evidence to the contrary?

Is it an issue you and your partner need to discuss and can resolve together?

Would discussing it with a professional trained to clarify and resolve such conflicts be your best option?

The best option for you is the one which gives the feeling of relief you're looking for, and ultimately the results you want.

Important Note: Ensure your unconscious blueprint™ is a nurturing, confident, adult one. The age, if within five to 10 years of your chronological age, is not as significant as the other characteristics. Does the image look like someone you would instinctively entrust your precious child to? If not, it needs updating before spending time and money on any other option.

Our relationships with others strongly influence our sense of identity, worthiness and well-being. Just as it is usually the ones we are closest to who bear the brunt of our unhappiness, it is their criticism or perceived lack of support that hurts the most. Let's explore how you can refresh your relationships with others, as well as yourself.

KEY POINTS

- » Unconscious fears can be blocking conception.
- » Modern stressors and the pain of choice tense your body.
- » Negative anchoring means you associate baby = pain, pregnant = pain.
- » The compounding effect of stories heard and media images is significant.
- » Awareness is the key to change.
- » Immerse yourself in positive experiences and images, and refuse to engage the negative.

*"You can have anything you want in life, just not everything.
Decide and make it into the right choice."*

Sue Lester

TWELVE.
RELATIONSHIPS REFRESHED

One of our primary needs is love, and the ensuing sense of security that comes from being connected to others. To a greater or lesser extent, we rely on others to reflect our value and worth back to us. It's that reflection from others, and a deeper knowing of self, which produces our unconscious blueprint™. In this chapter we explore the three main reasons relationships break down, some restorative / preventative measures, and guidelines to keep your keystone relationships refreshed and energising. Note: what applies to a spousal relationship can also apply to other relationships within the family, with friends, and in the workplace.

There can be many seemingly obvious reasons for relationships breaking down, but beneath the surface they all come back to just three root causes:

1. Conflicting values.

2. Unfulfilled love strategies.

3. Unloving unconscious blueprints of self and / or other.

Let's explore these in that order, as the unconscious blueprint can be influenced in a toxic way by the first two.

1. CONFLICTING VALUES

From reading Chapters 4 to 6 you understand that values represent what is important to us, so dictate how we spend our time, money and energy. Our power values are our true drivers and motivators, and an acknowledgement that we are balanced creatures of positive and negative. The key to understanding the impact of values in relationships is the awareness that in every individual, values shift and change over time. And no matter how close or co-dependant a relationship is, it still consists of two individuals with shifting values.

For example, when Jackie and Joe met, fun, freedom and adventure were high on both their values lists. They were perfectly suited to exploring adventurous destinations overseas, spending weekends trying abseiling, kayaking, orienteering, or having whole day love-ins, and partying often with their wide social circle. In their unconscious blueprints™ she was his gorgeous, sexy bundle of fun, and he was her adventure man with the cheeky grin – a perfect match.

As their lives unfolded, love, career, security and family started muscling their way to the top of their values. Fun, freedom and adventure were still there, but they didn't receive the same amount of time, energy and money as before. Priorities had shifted. Jackie and Joe had started talking about having children together, one day, generally after a glass or three of wine. Although they knew they hadn't been as careful as before, their unplanned pregnancy was a huge shock for them both. Jackie was loving her career and feeling like she was really starting to gain momentum. Joe loved the extra play money his career progression was producing and enjoyed driving his sporty car.

Suddenly a two-seater car was no longer practical so was sold to downsize the mortgage faster. They had to decide whose career was more important in the long-term for family finances, the importance of one of them spending time at home raising their baby rather than using day-care, and so many other decisions that arise when two are to become three.

There were value clashes right from the start of pregnancy. Jackie valued natural medicine's role in optimising pregnancy health enough to spend money on supplements Joe thought were a waste. Yet he willingly bought the most expensive off-road convertible baby pram after researching it as he would a new car. How to birth their baby and raise it afterwards identified many more value clashes as they each drew on their own family values in areas they had not formed strong adult views on.

Fortunately, because of the strength of their earlier relationship and the huge deposits they'd built up in their emotional bank accounts, they were able to negotiate their way through the upheavals. Joe was very much a hands-on dad, when he was home. Jackie slipped into her

'Mum' identity, and naturally her values shifted more quickly than Joe's, simply because of her daily routine caring for their child. It becomes more important to take your shoes off at the front door when you know your baby may pick up and eat whatever you have walked in. Getting the dishes quickly washed before sweeping the kitchen, after bathing, feeding and bedding baby, so you can finally sit down (phew!) becomes more important than your husband's need for sex in the kitchen. But not to him.

For their relationship to survive long-term he will need to start valuing Jackie in her new role, and reflecting on the importance of her career as primary carer of their child. It's also important he doesn't overdo that and see her only as 'Mum', ignoring her need for intellectual stimulation and to be seen as attractive and desirable by him. He must also acknowledge and allow for her personal husband / child-free time to recharge, alone and with her friends.

Values conflicts come to the fore in blended families, particularly when there are fundamental differences in parenting styles. Children can be caught in the tangled web of their old family values, their separated parents' newer values, the values of their step-parents, and the difference between what their step-siblings are used to and what they themselves see as important. No wonder they get confused, lost and act up. In the ideal situation their parents can agree on shared values for parenting, even if their personal values have changed. Successfully blending that with their new step-families takes time and concerted effort to achieve.

An example is Jill. She came to me to work out her new relationship issues before she and her fiancé moved in together with their respective children. Discipline is always a sticky point, in terms of who has the right to do what and whether the children will accept being corrected by the interloper. In Jill's case, pocket money became a sticking point. Jill's values dictated that her children did set chores around the house in return for their pocket money. If they didn't do those chores, they didn't get paid. If they spent their money very quickly, that was their choice and she wouldn't give them more. It was important to Jill that her children learnt the value of money and how to save.

On the other hand, her fiancé believed that children shouldn't be paid to do what they should automatically be doing, that is, doing their fair share around the home. He didn't give pocket money, but would buy whatever the children wanted. Those two very differing attitudes to pocket money had to be resolved into one system that both lots of children and parents could adjust to before moving in together.

In a situation like this there is never only one right way, and all options need to be negotiated after letting go of the idea that your way is the only right way. It is crucial to be able to recognise and compromise on things that are simply habits you've learnt from your parents, rather than strong values. For Jill, learning to earn and manage their own money was setting her children up for financial security later in life, so she wasn't prepared to compromise on that, and felt his children would benefit enormously too.

The solution came from recognising that being the main breadwinner of the family was high on Jack's values, and helping him see that he was actually denying his children the chance to learn the skills so they in-turn could fulfil that role in their own families. He also came to see that giving pocket money in no way diminished his importance as the family benefactor; he was simply allocating it in a different way. Jack also acknowledged that just because the children were meant to pull their own weight, it didn't mean that happened automatically, particularly once they became teenagers. Having consequences for not helping out, that is, the job not done and no pocket money, was an incentive for action.

An awareness of your own power values, those of your partner and children, can make an enormous difference to smooth communication in your home. The other key to even more loving relationships and harmonious homes is your love strategies.

> *"Worry never robs tomorrow of its sorrow.*
> *It only saps today of its joy."*
>
> *Leo Buscaglia*

2. UNFULFILLED LOVE STRATEGIES

The key to ongoing loving relationships is a simple strategy – a strategy of love which is so incredibly simple and powerful you wonder why everyone doesn't know about it and use it! It's obvious application is in romantic relationships, but can be equally potent when applied to children, extended family and the workplace.

Simply, every one of us is born with our own preferred strategy for giving and receiving love. As long as that strategy is fulfilled we will feel loved and forgive much more than we probably should! Firstly, in romantic relationships, and then we'll look at applying it to other relationships.

Strategies of love fall into four categories: visual, auditory, kinaesthetic and auditory digital.

Now, you may have heard these terms before, and perhaps already have a label for yourself, but please put that aside for the moment. Your preferred learning style, for example, does not automatically correlate with your innate preferred strategy for giving and receiving love. Bear in mind these are broad categories so not every aspect of a category will be meaningful to you.

For the visual, 'proof' of love comes in the form of gifts, of being taken places, a certain look in a lover's eyes, or seeing loving words written, whether on a card, email or SMS. Also in this category are acts of service, for example, washing your lover's car, keeping the house clean and tidy, cooking dinner, picking up dirty socks off the floor, and repairing that broken hinge. Beautifully wrapped birthday presents are usually non-negotiable for the Visuals, and they also value gifts that can be displayed either by being worn or as a decorative item. Note to men: whitegoods are rarely decorative, nor romantic.

For the auditory, 'proof' is in those famous three little words, "I love you", or in hearing their pet name or a special tone in their love's voice. Their idea of a perfect romantic date involves lots of talking, and they will often have "our song", a signature tune for the relationship. They want telephone calls not emails or texts, when apart from loved ones.

Auditory people will forgive and forget much if they are hearing the right words.

For the kinaesthetic, 'proof' is in being hugged, kissed, touched in a special place in a special way, and of course, sex. They will tend to want to have some form of body contact on a romantic date, for example, ankles entwined under the table, thighs touching sitting together, holding hands. Gifts that evoke a feeling, whether an experience (sky-diving as an extreme example) or that have a tactile element to it (a luxuriously soft scarf) connect.

Then there are the auditory-digital love strategists. They need to have a conversation in their head to decide whether they are feeling loved or not. They may come across as shy or distant, but potentially they are simply thinking it all through, deciding what your words and actions mean, and how to respond appropriately. Definitely not a good match for auditory love strategists, unless perhaps a highly narcissistic one who only loves the sound of his or her own voice.

And yes, of course you want them all, we all do! That's why falling in love is such an exciting and all-consuming process. When we first meet a potential partner we apply all the strategies to gain and hold their attention and 'love'. We go in with all guns blazing! It's when the relationship settles into a routine that things can go awry. When we get comfortable in a relationship we often allow ourselves to be distracted by work, children, TV, and other life issues. We then revert to the easiest strategy for us to give love, our own. Picking up those dirty socks is no longer done quite so lovingly. That's not an issue if our partner has exactly the same love strategy, but let's look at some examples where that isn't the case.

Keith is very much a visual strategist and shows his love by showering his partner, Vanessa, with gifts and clothes. He loves taking her out for surprise dinners, shows etcetera. Vanessa is kinaesthetic and loves cuddling on the lounge at home. Keith starts to feel unappreciated at her lack of enthusiasm at being seen out with him, and for his gifts to make up for not being home early every night. Vanessa is starting to feel he is buying her clothes because she's not good enough, not attractive enough, and starts to become suspicious about him not being home earlier. In her insecurity, Vanessa starts to increase her love strategy of physical contact. Keith starts to feel smothered, stops buying gifts, finds reasons to come home even later, and so on it goes.

On the other hand, Julie longs to receive gifts and says her husband, Jason, mustn't love her anymore because he never buys her flowers or takes her out. Jason is shocked to hear this, "What do you mean I don't love you? I told you so just this morning!". Visual versus auditory.

Then there is Amanda who, much to her family and friends' distress, allows Aaron to treat her like a doormat, simply because he often tells her how much he loves her. So, what to do?

Firstly you need to identify your own preferred strategy for giving and receiving love. Do this alone so you can be clear in your own mind, without your partner or someone else telling you what they think you are! Likewise, allow your partner to decide without help too. This can be quite an eye-opener for long-term couples, as over time one can accommodate and adapt to the other's strategy. And of course, no one likes to think they've had it all wrong for 25 years. It doesn't matter if you don't currently have a partner, because presumably you have friends or family. It's always a wise idea to get to know yourself and your needs better, isn't it?

Next step is to share your strategies with your partner and make a commitment to each other to always fulfil the other's strategy first. Of course, you can use yours as well, but their strategy is the priority for you. Now, no one is perfect, and you or your partner may occasionally need a gentle reminder of your needs. It's all about being loving, so pouting, moody silences, cranky voices etcetera aren't appropriate!

If you are in Amanda's situation or you are tolerating bad behaviour because the sex is amazing or she / he 'makes up' to you with gifts and outings, I strongly suggest you review your situation. When you allow yourself to move on you create space in your life for the genuinely loving relationship you deserve. It also frees your current loved one to find someone better suited to his / her needs.

For children it is important they experience feeling loved every day in many different ways, but they too have their own individual strategy for giving and receiving love. For younger children it is often easiest to observe how they show love – do they always want to be in physical contact with you whether cuddling, wrestling or sitting close? Does your child tell you in words, whether directly or by verbally sharing important things that happened that day? That's right, that chatterbox isn't being deliberately annoying, he's actually showering you with his love. Or are you often being given 'gifts' from the garden, a leaf, flower or drawings? It is especially important to visual children to see their pictures and handmade gifts displayed.

It is a matter of noticing what makes each child happiest, and ensuring that, at the very least, you show love in that way every day. You probably find your children are all different, but by consistently and frequently using their love strategies your home will quickly become much more harmonious. With practice you can be listening to your auditory child as you have an arm around your kinaesthetic and smiling at your visual. It also makes discipline so much easier, applying a stern tone of voice to the auditory child, and 'the eye' to the visual child etcetera.

It is important for teenagers, particularly kinaesthetic girls, to understand their own strategy for love. Just because it is being fulfilled doesn't mean it is true love, nor does it mean they should lower their standards and expectations and allow themselves to be treated disrespectfully. Actions and words must match.

In family dynamics it is often unfulfilled love strategies that cause the initial rift, so the easiest way back is through fulfilling love strategies and negotiating or acknowledging different or changed values. Remember too that unless you have shared this book and they have read it too, they won't suddenly start fulfilling your love strategy, unless you find a way to share with them what you need to. For a quick and easy to share resource, you can download my e-book, Win-Win Loving: Your Guide to Loving Relationships and Harmonious Homes, from my website www.growingcontent.com.au.

In the workplace, this can be applied by presenting the information as a personal development segment at a staff meeting. I did this at the national social enterprise organisation I was working for when I first started studying Neuro Linguistic Programming. Improvement in even one staff member's home life can impact greatly on the workplace atmosphere and productivity as a whole, and that was certainly the case after my very first presentation.

It is also a way of discovering each person's strategy so you know how to most effectively reward them. For example, would they prefer to be told they are doing a great job (auditory), get a physical pat on the shoulder or handshake (kinaesthetic), or see their name in a memo or newsletter (visual)? And yes, everyone loves a pay rise too, but just money isn't enough for most people. If you are struggling with a particular person, check in on your unconscious blueprint™ of him or her. Is it a likable image or not?

3. UNLOVING UNCONSCIOUS BLUEPRINT™

So, you and your partner have aligned your values, you're getting better at fulfilling each other's love strategies, but things still aren't getting back on track? Just as your own face within determines your self-esteem and behaviour, so too does your unconscious blueprint™ of your partner determine the health of your relationship. If you have an image of weakness, you will disempower your partner with your lack of respect and trust. On the other hand, if your image of your partner is overbearing, you'll disempower yourself.

Healthy relationships are ones in which two people stand as individuals, holding hands as a symbol of connection and support. Where one partner leans on the other, it eventually leads to resentment. Or when both lean on each other (co-dependant) to the point where one collapses so does the other, it is unhealthy for both.

Unhealthy versus Healthy Relationships

In Chapter 13 I discuss how to change your unconscious blueprint™, but for the moment start focussing on what you want to see or hear or feel from your partner. You've already proved you can easily notice when it's absent, and all that has done is create a negative anchor to your partner. In other words, you've taught yourself to associate unpleasant feelings with your partner, or at least part of his / her behaviour. Or perhaps you've anchored into your home, so as soon as you walk through the door you feel frustration or resentment. If it is fear, seek professional support now. Seriously.

So now it's time to turn those powers towards increasing your happiness instead of your unhappiness. Keep a sharp eye out for evidence that what you want already exists, highlight and reward it in your partner's love strategy immediately. Just as in training children and animals, the closer the reward to the action, the faster the learning. What you focus on increases, and that old adage, "You catch more flies with honey than with vinegar" is so true. Remember, the 'honey' is first and foremost your partner's love strategy, not yours, though you can throw that in as a bonus.

LINGUISTIC HAND GRENADES

If you want to really ignite an argument, toss in those linguistic hand grenades, "You always" and "You never". The sheer unfairness and wrongness of those generalisations 'always' and 'never' is guaranteed to wound. Not least because they are also indicating that you have 'never' noticed all the times they did try, albeit not to your standards, to meet your needs, to do that thing that is so important to you.

 **TIME TO CHANGE EXERCISE: DESIGNING YOUR IDEAL PARTNER**

Notice I didn't write 'perfect partner'? That's because, to my mind, there is no such thing as a perfect person. We are all simply human beings on a journey of growth, learning how to be the very best 'me' we each can be. And if you see your partner as perfect, what happens when he shows his human side – do you stop loving him? If he is perfect, don't you have to be also to be a worthy partner? Take the pressure off you both and aim for the ideal partner for you, warts'n'all.

If you are looking for a new partner or wondering if you are with the right one, here is an exercise to help you clarify what's important to you. Yes, it's those values popping up again, folks!

1. Down one side of a page list all of the essential qualities and characteristics of your ideal partner. Include tidy, if that's important to you. Some points to consider are faithful, trustworthy, same sense of humour and libido, likes animals, financially savvy, employed / business owner, 180 to 195 cm tall, healthy, good teeth, house-trained, intelligent, handyman, loves travel, can cook, hates watching TV sport, can talk footy to my dad, fashion-conscious, neat and tidy, can communicate his feelings etcetera. What does your ideal partner have? Remember to write what you want, not what you don't want. For example, replace "not a bully" with "respectful and kind".

2. Read through your list and consider. If he had all of those things, is there anything he could do or say that would cause you to walk away, such as lying? If so, add honesty to the list.

3. Highlight all your deal-breakers. Those are non-negotiable. For example, it's okay that he's not a tall, handsome cook, but he must absolutely be honest, faithful and financially secure.

4. If you have a partner or potential lined up, now go through and tick everything she / he has. If you hesitate on an item, score it out of 10 and move on. If definitely not present and no real potential, leave it blank.

5. If any of your deal breakers are blank or scoring low, there's the source of your doubt.

6. On the right hand side, write down all you have to offer to your ideal partner – yes, the universe expects a fair exchange. If you struggle to find your good qualities, it is a sign your self-esteem and self-image need adjusting. I strongly urge you to get yourself back on track before you look for a new partner, as you will only attract to the level you feel comfortable. So if you are feeling insecure, you will attract a bully. That's why you are still attracting the same man issues. If nothing changes, nothing changes, except perhaps hair colour and name.

7. Now go down your list and tick those that show up easily, and score yourself on those that could be strengthened.

8. Are there any qualities you feel you don't have at all, that your ideal partner would need to be happy? I suggest that if you look deeply enough inside, you will find them. They just need to be brought to light, dusted off and put into practice. What you recognise in others is already in you.

9. Time to consider the items in both lists that were scored. What actions can you take to strengthen those items? Is it time to discuss these findings with your partner?

Know that by working on improving your side of the equation there will always be a shift on the other side, a ripple-on effect. Not always what you might expect or hope for in the short-term, but definitely a shift. That's where boundary setting, in other words, retraining, becomes crucial to cement lasting change for yourself and others.

BOUNDARY SETTING

Effective boundary setting first and foremost involves a degree of self-belief and self-confidence. You need to be very clear in your own mind about exactly what you want to change, why, and the benefits to yourself and others. Then it is easier to communicate your new rules in a way they understand, and to be firm and consistent when they resist. Of course, there will be resistance from some. They have been very used to you prioritising their needs above yours, so it's initially inconsiderate, selfish, unloving of you to do so, but only in their eyes.

As long as you are firmly consistent, eventually they will accept, or choose not to and move on. Their choice doesn't automatically make yours wrong, except for them in their reality. It can still be 100 per cent right for you. Looking after your needs first isn't selfish. It's a very sensible way to ensure you always have enough (love, energy, patience) to give others as needed.

However, beware the energy vampires. They are those who will suck you dry if you let them, dragging you down into their Pity Pit. If you walk away from a visit feeling drained, know you have just visited with an energy vampire. By all means offer a helping hand up, but resist being dragged down as then you will both be stuck, wallowing in misery and helplessness. Be aware too of emotional blackmail being used to keep you close. One dear client who used to attract flocks of vampires bought herself a pretty silver cross on a chain to celebrate our work and her new confidence and boundaries. She used it as a resource anchor she could rub whenever an energy vampire was trying to be particularly invasive.

Sometimes the very best thing you can do to help yourself or someone else is to simply say, "No". And stick to it. (Even if it is your mother or child.)

KEY POINTS

» There are three main reasons relationships, marriages or friendships break down:

   a. Conflicting values – people change over time in different ways.

   b. Unfulfilled love strategies – not feeling loved by the way the partner demonstrates love.

   c. Unloving unconscious blueprint™ of each other – unconscious disempowerment.

» The only person you can change is you, but there will be a flow-on effect.

» Boundary setting needs self-belief and self-confidence, and is essential to a healthy relationship.

» Sometimes saying "No" is the very best thing you can do, for yourself and others.

RELATIONSHIPS REFRESHED

"And the day came when the risk to remain tight in the bud was more painful than the risk it took to blossom."

Anais Nin

THIRTEEN.
NEXT STEPS: HOW TO LET GO AND GROW

It's time to change, if you're ready to let go and grow. Here you can adjust your personal time stream into its optimum position for you. You can choose the efficient or relax mode, depending on your needs during the day. I'll explain how you can update your unconscious blueprint™ and review the key points of each chapter. Consider this your own executive summary!

If you skipped the Essential Pre-reading Exercise before Chapter 1, please go back and do it now. Otherwise this chapter won't make sense.

"The way to get started is to quit talking and begin doing."

Walt Disney

OPTIMISING YOUR TIME STREAM

Over the years, working with hundreds of individual clients I've found there is an optimum position for your time stream. You are aware from the pre-reading exercise where yours is positioned, the direction of your past and future, and whether your time stream touches your body or not. You may have a clear or vague sense of what form and colour it has. Note that your time stream may have already adjusted if you made some deep, unconscious shifts while working through the book exercises and thinking about what you were reading. It is entirely up to you whether you adjust yours if it doesn't match the following, and you can always change it back again if you don't like the changes you create. Read through to the end of this section then close your eyes to follow the instructions.

I've found the optimum position for your past is behind you, though not directly behind. Behind the left or right shoulder enables you to glance back to get any learning you need refreshing, without taking full focus off your future. You'll know whether left or right is best for you, and either is perfectly fine.

It probably won't surprise you now that if the optimum position for your past is behind, then your future works best stretching out directly in front of you as far as you can see. Your whole body is in alignment with moving forward.

TIME TO CHANGE EXERCISE: TIME STREAM ADJUSTMENT

When you are ready to make the change, close your eyes and get a clear sense of your own time stream. As you observe it, know it is yours and you can change it. Any changes you make will stay locked in place until you choose to change it again. In your mind's eye, plus physically if you wish, move your past around until it is behind one of your shoulders, just so you can comfortably glance back for a learning without losing focus on the present and future. Then move your future so it stretches way out in front of you, as far as you can see. Set the intention to lock these changes in place, clapping your hands together loudly once. At this point you may notice a shift in colour and / or a change in form. Some people don't. Simply observe without judgement. Notice if your time stream is touching you, including going through you, in any place.

Make your change now, if you wish.

EFFICIENT VS. RELAXED

If you struggle to relax, to be in the moment after working efficiently during the day, your time stream is most likely not touching you. If you can easily get lost in the moment, so consequently seem to constantly be rushing around in catch-up mode, then your time stream is likely to be going through you, or at least touching you. Some people naturally and automatically adjust their time streams throughout the day without conscious awareness. If that is you, great, you don't need to change a thing. That is the aim of re-training yourself by consciously adjusting whether your time stream touches you or not. Eventually it will become automatic for you.

All you need to do to change to be more efficient is close your eyes, get a sense of your time stream, and either step out or pull it out to the side, whichever feels right for you. Likewise, if you need to relax or be more creative, then you'll want to step into or pull your time stream over to touch your body. If you get into a routine of changing on arrival and departure at work, including sitting in your home office, then you'll get to the unconscious competence faster. You'll also be more relaxed driving in peak hour traffic or on public transport. Play around with it to find what works best for you.

HOW TO CHANGE YOUR UNCONSCIOUS BLUEPRINT™

Review what you wrote in the pre-reading exercise about the unconscious blueprint™ of yourself. I'll firstly explain the differences in internal images and what else you can do to support change before sharing one way to update your unconscious blueprint™ by yourself.

> *1. If your unconscious blueprint™ is considerably younger (or older) than your chronological age, particularly if it's not a positive image*, then absolutely you'll want to update it as soon as possible. Doing so will make a significant difference to your life. If while doing the process in this book yourself you find your blueprint changes in increments, for example, from six years old to 14 years old to late 20's to now, know that's perfectly fine. It is also possible to change in one jump. If you prefer to seek out a Master NLP practitioner / coach to guide the process for you, ask them to use a sub-modality shift as in a belief change (show her this book),

which is what I use one-on-one with clients. Or you can contact me directly for a telephone session. You may find significant shifts in your relationships afterwards and will need to clarify and maintain new boundaries with some who may resist your new confidence.

2. If your unconscious blueprint™ is approximately your age now, but with an unhappy, disempowered appearance, then it's time to identify how you want to look and feel instead so you know what to change to. What can you do to create your personal transformation? What is it you need to change to do differently? Know you can't change anyone else; only influence them with your own changes. What help or tools do you need to transition more easily? Are you ready to work with a head transition coach for ongoing mindset shifts, support and accountability? At the very least, re-read this book, doing all the exercises, and find ways you apply it in your own life every day, one step at a time.

3. If your unconscious blueprint™ is approximately your age now, with a happy confident image that you feel doesn't match your reality, you don't need to change that image, just your focus. Shift your focus to tune into all the examples of what is going well in your life. Get your RAS (Reticular Activating System) filtering for what you *do* want. If you are focussing on the negative, that's all you'll see, hear and feel. Tune into a different station, shine your torch on what you want to see. Notice all you could be grateful for, and notice your emotional state change. That state change flows on to your physiology, your behaviour, and therefore your results. Write 10 things in your gratitude journal before bed every night.

This also applies if you have relationship struggles at home or at work. Focus on what you want to see and hear, and generally people will respond with that behaviour – it's like catching kids being good. As you've probably found, the more you point out what you don't like, the more you notice it, and the more irritated the other person gets.

4. If your unconscious blueprint™ is of you now, or slightly younger, happy and confident and that matches your reality – great! That's exactly where you want to be. You can use this knowledge to increase your awareness in your relationships with others, the dynamics in families and workplaces, and facilitate changes. Note that 'slightly' younger means less than 10 years if you are 40 plus, less than five years if 30 plus, and within a year if 20 plus, otherwise you miss the wisdom and extra confidence of those missing years of life experience.

5. When you have relationship difficulties, check what your unconscious blueprint™ of that person is. Are you overly empowering him / her, or disempowering him / her? You can update that image to one that serves you more, a realistic one without emotional charge. If your unconscious blueprint™ is already neutral, then consider how the person involved might be picturing you? How can you communicate in a way they understand, to diffuse the situation? (For example, love language). Or is it simply time to move on as your values no longer match and both of you aren't willing to renegotiate or compromise?

TIME TO CHANGE EXERCISE: THE CHANGE PROCESS

Now that you are ready to change, you'll need a mirror, or a fairly recent photo of yourself that you like. If using a mirror, if you normally feel better wearing makeup, apply it now. Ensure your hair is clean and tidy and you are wearing clothes you love. I recommend you read through the following instructions several times so you can do what you need to, without referring to the book too often.

You'll need to be able to see in your mind's eye your new empowering image to make the change. To do that, look into the mirror or photo. Notice your hair style, the amount of hair, and whether it is dyed to hide the grey or not. Notice your eyebrows, the shape of your jaw, the texture of your skin. Look at your mouth, notice the corners up, down or neutral. If you are looking in the mirror, make your mouth smile at least a little. Notice all of the changes that reflect you are older and wiser now. Look into your eyes, the window to your soul. They are adult eyes that have seen pain and joy, love and lust, and they reflect your journey to this point.

Now close your eyes and bring up that mirror image or photo. Open your eyes, study the mirror or photo more, close your eyes, bring up the image. Keep doing this until when you close your eyes you can see a fairly clear desired image. You are now ready.

Close your eyes and see your desired image. Step into the image so you are looking through your own eyes, noticing the bright colours around you, hearing the sounds around you, and feeling how great it feels to be the ideal you. Turn up those feelings, making them so strong you can feel them bubbling through you.

Now step out of the picture so you can see yourself, the ideal you, in the picture again.

Open your eyes.

This time close your eyes and bring up your unconscious blueprint, the one you wish to change. As you look at that image, make the 'ideal you' image appear small and quite dark in the lower left hand corner of the screen of your mind.

Now, as you explode that new image big and bright across the screen of your mind, the old image shrinks and fades into the lower left hand corner. You've switched them. Open your eyes.

Keep repeating this, starting each time with the old image on the screen, and the new down in the bottom left corner. Faster and faster, as fast as one, two, three ... about 10 times. When you can no longer bring up your old image, you've done it. Congratulations!

You can follow the same process when you are changing your unconscious blueprint™ of someone else, such as your husband or colleague.

If you prefer to have expert assistance please email info@growingcontent.com.au to arrange your time to change, wherever you live in the world.

Note to Master NLP Practitioners / Coaches: I described a modified Swish Pattern above as it can be done at home by readers. In my own practice I prefer to use a detailed sub-modality change process.

To conclude, for now, what follows is a summary of the key points from each chapter to make it easier for you to review what you've read. The more you use the exercises and techniques, the more automatically you'll use them as needed, the more on track and content you'll be. However, set yourself up for success by choosing just one thing to start focussing on, not everything all at once. Master that and then add in the next change. Starting with keeping your mindset in the present, self-talk, self-worth and self-forgiveness will make a huge difference, and then any excess weight, relationship issues, career confusion etcetera are more easily resolved.

I've also included a list, by no means exhaustive, of resources I've found useful, as you might too. I welcome your feedback, questions and success stories, so feel free to email me or post on my Facebook or LinkedIn pages.

Know you are worthy. You are enough. You are loved. Everything you need is inside, you just need to learn how to ask, listen and act. It only takes one step at a time to get you to where you want to be now. Note the habit of improvement is more important than the rate. Your journey is one of continual growth, not a race to (imaginary) perfection. However, life is too short to waste tripping over head trash. Let go and grow.

KEY POINTS

- » **The optimum position for your time stream is with the past behind your shoulder and your future stretching out directly in front of you.**
- » **To be more relaxed or creative, have your time stream going through you or at least touching you. For more efficiency have it beside you, not touching your body.**
- » **Different variations of your unconscious blueprint™ require different adjustments**
- » **It is essential to have a clear image of what you wish your new unconscious blueprint™ to be before changing.**
- » **Everything you need is inside, you just need to learn how to ask, listen and act.**
- » **Life is too short to waste tripping over head trash. Let go and grow, one step at a time.**

"A problem is just the temporary absence of the right thought."

Sue Lester

KEY POINT SUMMARY

Chapter 1 The Inspiration: The Face Within Revealed

» You have an unconscious blueprint™ which can be affecting your life negatively. Changing your unconscious blueprint™ changes your self-esteem and confidence.

» Your unconscious blueprint™ of others dictates your relationship with them.

» Guilt chains you to your past.

Chapter 2 Stories of Changing Faces

» Your unconscious blueprint™ can be delaying conception, stifling your business growth, sabotaging your relationships, and leaving you vulnerable to abuse.

» Labels are disempowering. No one or no thing is 'just a ...'.

Chapter 3 Introducing Your Captain and Crew

» For smooth sailing through life, your captain (conscious mind) and crew (unconscious mind) must be in alignment.

» Memories, beliefs and your unconscious blueprint™ are stored as images in your unconscious mind.

» It is possible to have more than one unconscious blueprint™ of yourself.

Chapter 4 Whose World Is It? Mapping Your Reality

» Everyone has a different reality, based on how they filter the information flooding their senses.

» It's the meaning you give to an event, not the event itself, that makes the difference.

- » Expecting others to filter information exactly the same way as you sets you up for hurt.
- » Question: How can he do / say that? Answer: Because he / she is not me.
- » Values and memories are two of the strongest filters which create your reality.
- » The past and future only exist in your imagination. The only real moment is the present.
- » Anxiety control: "What if it doesn't happen like that? How will that feel?"
- » You can learn to control your imagination, therefore your past, present and future.
- » Positive thinking 100 per cent of the time is unrealistic, and trying is depressing.
- » The Two No Rule helps with setting new boundaries and disciplining children.
- » Language is what we use to explain what we experience to ourselves and others. It creates our individual realities.

Chapter 5 Reclaiming Your Personal Power (Inc. Financial Freedom)

- » Living in your personal power you are calm, confident, centred, you know who you are, you like who you are, you know where you're heading, and have faith in your ability to get there.
- » Living At Effect you are playing the victim, giving your responsibility, and therefore power, away by blaming others, the past and the future. Focussing on excuses not results, staying stuck. Telling yourself you can't help eating chocolate biscuits instead of fruit, when all you need to do is stop buying the biscuits.
- » Living At Cause you are powerful, taking full responsibility for your own actions, meaning and emotional state, and the results produced. You live in the present where you can create the future you desire.

Chapter 6 Power Values: Your True Drivers

» Your values are simply what is most important to you.
» How you spend your time and money indicates your top values.
» Your power values, your 'dark' side, are your true drivers.
» Honouring and harnessing your power values to your goals gets results faster, while also fulfilling your 'golden' values.

Chapter 7 Putting The 'I' Back Into Your LIFE

» Balanced people have both positive and negative traits.
» A positive trait can be negative in some circumstances, and vice versa.
» Remember that others ultimately benefit from you being the very best, happiest, fulfilled you possible.
» Until you know and love who you are, you will never be content.
» Live your life, not someone else's version of what it should be, or what you think someone else thinks it should be.

Chapter 8 De-Stress For Success

» Three underlying causes of stress / overwhelm:
  1. Lack self-worth
  2. Lack self-trust
  3. Not living in the present
» Three layers of de-stressing effectively:
  1. Physical
  2. Emotional
  3. Mindset
» Practical strategies:
  1. Breathe 3:6
  2. Senses walk

3. And what if it doesn't? How would that feel? (Quality Questions.)

4. Acknowledge and reward

» The only person you can change is yourself, however, there will be a ripple on effect to others.

» The only person you need to forgive is yourself.

Chapter 9 Pain and Dis-ease

» The placebo effect is evidence of the strong mind-body connection in creating and healing dis-ease and pain.

» Secondary gain is the underlying benefit of having an apparently negative issue.

» The secondary gain must be identified and replaced with an alternative before true healing occurs.

» Pain is your body's way of communicating that something is not right, and needs attention.

» Repressing strong emotion causes dis-ease in your body.

» Loss + Guilt + Relief = Grief

» Balancing out the positives and negatives of a death will give you peace of mind.

» You always have a choice; you just might not like the consequences.

» Life is too short to spend with someone who wants to change you to suit them.

» The only person you ever need to forgive is yourself.

Chapter 10 Weighing Heavily On Your Mind

» There can be underlying emotional and psychological reasons for excess weight.

» Self-protection provides a physical and emotional buffer.

- » Self-abuse confirms own negative self-identity.
- » Family fat – generational poor habits and emotional connection to food.
- » Remember 'exercise' is movement. Use it or lose it.
- » Aim for the healthiest version of your body, not someone else's.
- » Utilise the power of language with encouraging self-talk, and 'release' your excess weight.

Chapter 11 Infertility: Are You Unconsciously Blocking Conception?

- » Unconscious fears can be blocking conception.
- » Modern stressors and the pain of choice tense your body.
- » Negative anchoring means you associate baby = pain, pregnant = pain.
- » The compounding effect of stories heard and media images is significant.
- » Awareness is the key to change.
- » Immerse yourself in positive experiences and images, and refuse to engage the negative.

Chapter 12 Relationships Refreshed

- » There are three main reasons relationships, marriages or friendships, break down:
   a. Conflicting values – people change over time in different ways.
   b. Unfulfilled love strategies – not feeling loved by the way the partner demonstrates love.
   c. Unloving unconscious blueprint™ of each other – unconscious disempowerment.
- » The only person you can change is you, but there will be a flow-on effect.

- » Boundary setting needs self-belief and self-confidence, and is essential to a healthy relationship.
- » Sometimes saying "No" is the very best thing you can do, for yourself and others.

Chapter 13 Next Steps: How To Let Go and Grow

- » The optimum position for your time stream is with the past behind your shoulder and your future stretching out directly in front of you.
- » To be more relaxed or creative, have your time stream going through you or at least touching you. For more efficiency, have it beside you, not touching your body.
- » Different variations of your unconscious blueprint™ require different adjustments
- » It is essential to have a clear image of what you wish your new unconscious blueprint™ to be before trying to change.
- » Everything you need is inside, you just need to learn how to ask, listen and act.
- » Life is too short to waste tripping over head trash. Let go and grow, one step at a time.

KEY POINT SUMMARY

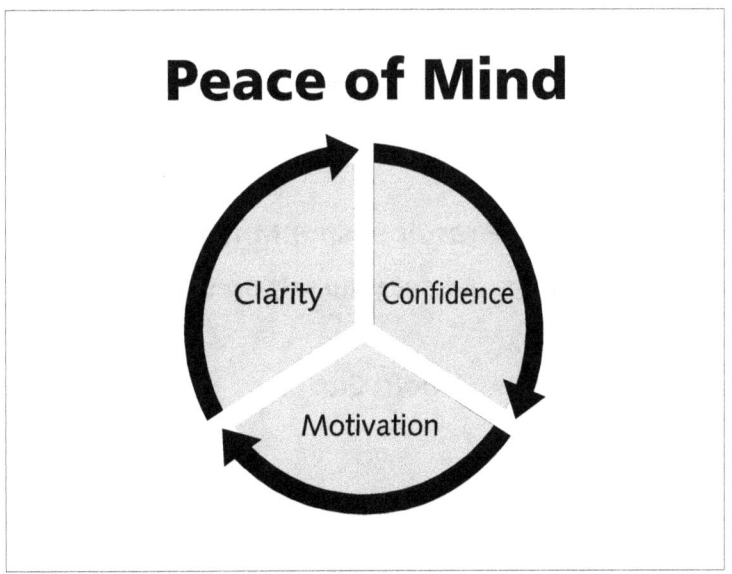

"Success isn't the result of spontaneous combustion. You must set yourself on fire."

Arnold Glasgow

REFERENCES & RECOMMENDATIONS

Bandler, Richard *Guide To Transformation* Health Communications Florida, 2008

Bays, Brandon *The Journey* Element Edition, 2003

Brockman, Howard *Dynamic Energetic Healing* Columbia Press, 2006

Buckley, Dr Sarah J. *Gentle Birth, Gentle Mothering* One Moon Press, 2005

Cameron, Julia *The Artist's Way* Pan Books, 1995

Chapman, Gary *The Five Love Languages* Strand Publishing, 2004

Chopra, Deepak *Ageless Body, Timeless Mind* Rider, 1993

Clason, George S. *The Richest Man In Babylon* Penguin Group Australia, 2002

Coelho, Paulo *The Alchemist* Harper San Francisco, 1994

Csikszentmihalyi, Mihaly *Flow* Harper Perennial Modern Classics Edition, 2008

Dalai Lama, His Holiness The *The Art Of Happiness* Hodder Australia, 1998

Demartini, Dr John F. *How To Make One Hell Of A Profit And Still Get To Heaven* Hay House, 2004

Doidge, Norman *The Brain That Changes Itself* Penguin Books, 2007

Gawler, Dr Ian *Peace Of Mind* Michelle Anderson Publishing, 2002

Gerber, Michael E. *The EMyth Enterprise* Harper Collins, 2009

Hicks, Esther and Jerry (The Teachings of Abraham) *Ask And It Is Given* Hay House, 2004

Hill, Napolean *Think & Grow Rich* Ballantine Books Edition, 1983

Johnson, Dr Spencer *Who Moved My Cheese?* Vermillion London, 1999

Laborde, Genie Z. *Influencing With Integrity* Crown House Publishing, 1998

Lipton, Bruce H. *The Biology Of Belief* Hay House, 2010

Lipton, Bruce H. & Bhaerman, Steve *Spontaneous Evolution* Hay House, 2011

Lundin, Stephen C., Paul, Harry and Christensen, John *Fish!* Omnibus Hodder and Stoughton, 2006

Mongan, Marie F. *Hypno Birthing The Mongan Method* Health Communications USA 2005

O'Connor, Joseph & Lages, Andrea *Coaching With NLP* Element UK, 2004

O'Connor, Joseph *Free Yourself From Fears* Nicholas Brealey Publishing 2005

Prior, Robin & O'Connor, Joseph *NLP & Relationships* Element UK, 2000

Sharma, Robin *The Monk Who Sold His Ferrari* Harper Collins, 2012

Sherwood, Dr Patricia *Emotional Literacy* ACER Press Australia, 2008

Slater, Zoe *Kids Or No Kids?* Book Pal, 2012

Thomson, Garner with Khan, Dr Khalid *Magic In Practice Introducing Medical NLP* Hammersmith Press London, 2008

Tolle, Eckhart *The Power Of Now* Hodder Australia, 2004

Weir, Bert with Charlie Scandrett *You Were Born Special, Beautiful and Wonderful, What Happened?* Weir Knightsbridge and Associates, 1993

Whitecloud, William *The Magician's Way* New World Library Edition, 2009

REFERENCES & RECOMMENDATIONS

"All that we are is a result of what we have thought."

Dhammapada

TESTIMONIALS

"Sue Lester is a true catalyst of change. She knows precisely how to make your life the extraordinary adventure you deserve."

Benjamin J. Harvey, founder of Authentic Education

www.authenticeducation.com.au

"It's all due to changing my six-year-old image (unconscious blueprint™). I used to feel like I was looking up to everyone in a room, and now I feel on the same level. I've gone from never driving more than 30 minutes by myself to driving alone on a four-hour trip to check myself into a hotel, set up and run an expo stand, and present my message from stage. I was able to speak to my father on the telephone without the usual stomach knotting anxiety I've felt for years. I felt fine. Now my husband and I are planning our first overseas holiday together in 32 years and it's exciting, not stressful!"

Jane Marin, owner / principal, Golden Isis – Inspired Energy.

www.goldenisis.com.au

"When I first met Sue I knew she was the type of person I could trust and rely on to give me unbiased personal and business advice. Sue has a great way of making you look at life from a bird's eye perspective, which is really important, especially if you find you are a bit side-tracked in life. I'm glad I have someone like Sue to guide me through it all. I know I'm still in my early stages of becoming the person I want to be, but I know that when I succeed Sue will definitely have played a big part in helping me achieve my goals."

James Hay, Fused Air-conditioning.

www.fusedair.com.au

"Before working with Sue I had been juggling the decision to fully jump into my own business and let go of the safety rope that was paid employment. A year later I am living my love, working in my business, balancing my passion as a coach and my passion as a mum, and getting to do what I love whilst making a difference every day. Coaching with Sue gave me the tools, the commitment, the accountability and the cheer squad to go out and do what I knew I always wanted to do, but I didn't quite believe in myself enough. I've since realised those safety lines were holding me back and I now look for the vines that will swing me into the next adventure."

Monique Longhurst, ASPIRE Personal Development and Consulting, and Aspiring Women.

www.aspireinfo.com.au

"I find it difficult to fully express the amazing changes that Sue Lester and her coaching techniques have helped bring to my life. Sue is the ultimate life coach who has been able to help guide me through both personal and business issues and arm me with techniques to deal with future issues when they arise. Her coaching has made such a difference to my outlook on life and the challenges it throws, my relationships, both personally and professionally, and my overall health and well-being. Sue has the amazing ability to say just what I need to hear in a wonderfully practical and no-nonsense way. The thought of not investing in my well-being and future direction is now just so foreign. I truly believe that if more people embraced NLP and Sue's coaching techniques, the world would be a better place."

Cara Phillips, director & creator Carmaje Skincare

www.carmaje.com.au

TESTIMONIALS

"With so much going on in life, getting clarity and focus was extremely difficult, and then Growing Content came along. The head transition coach at Growing Content has kept me focused for over 12 months now and both my business and personal life have not been better. The ability to have Sue Lester to keep me accountable has been amazing. I can highly recommend her services."

Nathan McDonald, founder and business instructor, Black Belt Business.

www.blackbeltbusiness.com.au

"Thank you, Sue, for taking the time to talk to me at the BBB Massive Planning Day 2012 and realising I needed help to clear the head trash. In the 12 months we have worked together I have grown in confidence. I speak up when I need to speak up, control emotions through negotiations, and have dealt with some deep personal issues. I am using portion control (most of the time) when eating, drinking less booze, and have taken up Hapkido and other exercise. I am feeling better in myself and I have learnt to trust. Most importantly, I have a far better relationship with my beautiful wife and children. Thank you so much."

Ian Simeon, director, Unity Glass Pty Ltd

"I always look forward to my NLP coaching sessions with Sue. Her knowledge and life experience means we can get to the essence of an issue – without having to go into the story of everything. NLP is wonderful in that the processes used by Sue deal with our underlying mental / emotional conditioning and programming – which is often the cause of how we feel or respond to circumstances unfolding on our lives. In our adult years, this programming frequently no longer serves us and NLP assists with finding new strategies and perspectives to create for ourselves the life we want. As an added bonus, these sessions also assist in developing a deeper understanding of whom we are and connection with ourselves. I would highly recommend Sue Lester – whether trying to unravel hurt and trauma from the past or whether you are open to looking for the triggers that you have in sabotaging your happiness now, in business or your personal life – or both!"

Veronica Mander, natural health practitioner

"I have been working with Sue Lester for the past 12 months on a number of focus areas. Two years ago I was 'a little lost in transition' moving from 24 years in a corporate role to establishing and growing my own small business and all that comes with that. I was in a little overwhelm at all the hats I was once wearing and decided on key focus areas with Sue – methods to improve my work / life balance, including setting long and short-term goals, taking time out each week for myself, and letting go of 'the small stuff' that was holding me back. The NLP visualisation sessions were fantastic and provided me with clarity on what my key next steps were. The most exciting part was revisiting my Success Map Wheel after 12 months to recognise the areas I had made the most progress with."

Terri Cave, founding leader of Your Inspiration At Home

"I have had the pleasure of having Sue as a friend and colleague, which means every now and again when I was feeling really 'human' and not very 'healer', Sue would offer me a session. Sue has a wonderful gift for challenging your perspectives on things; she also has a gift for believing in people and accepting them for who they are. I found myself being able to trust her with my stuff and allowing myself to surrender to her process. Each time I have noticed something positive shift: either I have felt better or perhaps gained an insight in to a different perspective which opened another door of possibility and helped me feel less stuck. Definitely a woman I respect and treasure."

Lisa Cutforth, nutritionist and lifestyle transformation coach

www.IveGotLife.com.au

www.RightSizeYourWeight.com.au

TESTIMONIALS

"I have known Sue for over 15 years. She is an inspirational coach and a lover of life, who truly walks her talk. Her passion to inspire and assist people to make positive changes in their lives comes straight from her heart and is a driver of her success. She aspires to be the best person she can and is committed to her own journey of living a life of excellence. Her love for travel and new challenges ensure she is always evolving and growing. Sue is a person who you will feel safe with and at ease; whilst she helps you smooth your path through life."

Mandy Napier BSc, mindset specialist, coach and speaker

www.mindsetforsuccess.com.au

"The aim of life is self-development. To realise one's nature perfectly, that is what each of us is here for."

Oscar Wilde

ABOUT THE AUTHOR

Sue Lester BA DipTeach. Master Practitioner NLP, Hypnosis, Neurological Re-patterning, Master Results Coach

During more than 20 years exploring remote areas across the globe and working in education and social enterprise, the one thing that stood out for Sue Lester was that the only thing really stopping people from moving forward is their mindset. From Cairo to Kathmandu, London to Washington, Buenos Aires to Brisbane, Sue found people achieving amazing results despite the odds, and those who didn't despite their advantages. Sue realised if she helped you change your mindset, you can change your world.

So Sue started her business, Growing Content: Smoothing Your Path, so she could more easily be a catalyst of change, helping people change their mindsets so they can dissolve their boundaries and transform their lives, free from overwhelm and self-doubt. Her head transition coaching three-step program, Let Go and Grow, will give you absolute clarity, authentic confidence and inspired motivation. Free from the head trash of the past you'll be living fully in the present, creating that future you truly desire and deserve right now.

Sue Lester is a key note speaker, educator, Head Transition Coach and Master Practitioner of Neuro Linguistic Programming, Hypnosis and Neurological Re-patterning. Sue firmly believes in holistic well-being, and the power of the mind-body connection.

She developed and runs The Personal Power Transformation program, De-Stress For Success workshops and retreats, plus numerous in-house training programs for a variety of organisations, from social enterprise to accountancy firms. Topics in demand include: The Impact of Your Unconscious Blueprint on Workplace Dynamics, De-Stress For Success, Self Leadership First: Re-programming Yourself for Success, and Communication With Connection.

In demand as a guest speaker, Sue has inspired and entertained groups from five to 550, and is looking forward to sharing her story and learning with thousands more. Sue also writes regularly for a number of magazines, blogs and forums, and between 2011 and 2012 hosted her own weekly radio program, Let Go And Grow With Sue Lester. Somewhere in all of that, Sue makes time to de-stress herself with bush and beach walks, adventurous travel with her partner, Peter, and that food of the gods, chocolate.

Sue's most popular speaking topics are:

Head Trash in Business: The Impact of Your Unconscious Blueprint on Workplace Dynamics

Ditch The Bitch: Turning Self-Sabotage Into Self-Motivation.

De-Stress For Success: The True Underlying Causes of Stress and Practical Ways to Change.

Talk Yourself Into Success: Changing How You Think and Feel About Public Speaking.

Personal Power: How To Put The 'I' Back Into Your LIFE

You can connect with Sue Lester by:

Phone: +61 7 3103 2679

Skype: Sue Lester Growing Content (please email to introduce yourself before sending a Skype request otherwise it will be ignored – too much spam these days!)

Email: info@growingcontent.com.au

Post: Growing Content Pty Ltd

P.O. Box 969, Redcliffe Qld 4020, Australia

Facebook: www.facebook.com/GrowingContentSmoothingYourPath

Linked In: http://au.linkedin.com/in/suelester/

Web: (Speaker Kit available): www.growingcontent.com.au

ABOUT THE AUTHOR

BONUS: If you are keen for more clarity, confidence and motivation, book in for your one-hour Success Map session. In this session you'll measure where you are across your life, identify your key focus areas, and map out your path to success. The special The Face Within reader price is $90 (normally $185). There are four offered each month, and they can be conducted via Skype worldwide. Add an extra $90 if you want to include a 30-minute unconscious blueprint™ update with your Success Map session (normally $125). Please mention this special offer when booking.

"Whatever you think you can do or believe you can do, begin it. Action has a magic, grace, and power in it."

Goethe

NAKURU HOPE

$1 from each copy of this book sold will be donated to Nakuru Hope.

www.nakuruhope.org

Making a difference to another life, a community, the world, can be achieved. In 2008, Western Australian Susan Saleeba decided to make a difference to those women and children merely surviving on hope in the slums of Kaptembwa, Nakuru, Kenya. She took action, and continues despite the odds to make her vision a reality.

Changing a life, breaking the circle of destitution comes through education. Nakuru Hope allows those who are educated at the Learning Centre to have a voice, to regain their respect, and to have the knowledge that someone does care.

Nakuru Hope believes that everyone is entitled to a safe family environment, where those children are orphaned or abandoned are given the essentials of life: love, food, medical assistance and education.

Nakuru Hope ensures that those who wish to help can travel and volunteer without huge costs usually associated with volunteer services.

Take an inspiring journey through **www.nakuruhope.org** and discover how you too can make a difference.

● ● ● ● ●

THE FACE WITHIN

NEXT RELEASES

The Face Within: How To Change Your Unconscious Blueprint

- E-Book available on Amazon 2013
- Companion Workbook available from www.growingcontent.com.au 2013
- Audio Program Series, including Change Process Recordings, available from www.growingcontent.com.au 2013

The Face Within Business Edition: How unconscious blueprints turn workplaces into schoolyards

This edition focuses on the impact of your unconscious blueprint™ of yourself and others in the workplace. Whether you are struggling with staff clashes making your workplace resemble a schoolyard, or a small business owner struggling to push through your own limitations, unconscious blueprints™ could be the source of the pain. Re-program yourself for success first, then create changes to shift office politics all the way through to company culture.

Enquiries, including in-house training options, to

info@growingcontent.com.au.

The Global Adventures of a Bundy Chick: Dumping Head Trash, Australia to Zanzibar

These are all the stories Sue Lester didn't write home about! Wavering on that line between courageous and down-right stupid, this irreverent and humorous collection of travel stories will delight anyone who's ever thrown on a backpack, or preferred just to watch.

Expected release September 2014.

www.ingramcontent.com/pod-product-compliance
Lightning Source LLC
Chambersburg PA
CBHW052018290426
44112CB00014B/2287